W9-BFG-617

Scott Foresman SCIENCE

Series Authors

Dr. Timothy Cooney
*Professor of Earth Science and
 Science Education*
Earth Science Department
University of Northern Iowa
Cedar Falls, Iowa

Michael Anthony DiSpezio
Science Education Specialist
Cape Cod Children's Museum
Falmouth, Massachusetts

Barbara K. Foots
Science Education Consultant
Houston, Texas

Dr. Angie L. Matamoros
Science Curriculum Specialist
Broward County Schools
Ft. Lauderdale, Florida

Kate Boehm Nyquist
Science Writer and Curriculum Specialist
Mount Pleasant, South Carolina

Dr. Karen L. Ostlund
Professor
Science Education Center
The University of Texas at Austin
Austin, Texas

Contributing Authors

Dr. Anna Uhl Chamot
*Associate Professor and
 ESL Faculty Advisor*
Department of Teacher Preparation
 and Special Education
Graduate School of Education
 and Human Development
The George Washington University
Washington, D.C.

Dr. Jim Cummins
Professor
Modern Language Centre and
 Curriculum Department
Ontario Institute for Studies in Education
Toronto, Canada

Gale Philips Kahn
Lecturer, Science and Math Education
Elementary Education Department
California State University, Fullerton
Fullerton, California

Vincent Sipkovich
Teacher
Irvine Unified School District
Irvine, California

Steve Weinberg
Science Consultant
Connecticut State
 Department of Education
Hartford, Connecticut

Scott Foresman

Editorial Offices: Glenview, Illinois • Parsippany, New Jersey • New York, New York
Sales Offices: Parsippany, New Jersey • Duluth, Georgia • Glenview, Illinois
Carrollton, Texas • Ontario, California
www.sfscience.com

Content Consultants

Dr. J. Scott Cairns
National Institutes of Health
Bethesda, Maryland

Jackie Cleveland
Elementary Resource Specialist
Mesa Public School District
Mesa, Arizona

Robert L. Kolenda
Science Lead Teacher, K-12
Neshaminy School District
Langhorne, Pennsylvania

David P. Lopath
Teacher
The Consolidated School District
of New Britain
New Britain, Connecticut

Sammantha Lane Magsino
Science Coordinator
Institute of Geophysics
University of Texas at Austin
Austin, Texas

Kathleen Middleton
Director, Health Education
ToucanEd
Soquel, California

Irwin Slesnick
Professor of Biology
Western Washington University
Bellingham, Washington

Dr. James C. Walters
Professor of Geology
University of Northern Iowa
Cedar Falls, Iowa

Multicultural Consultants

Dr. Shirley Gholston Key
Assistant Professor
University of Houston-Downtown
Houston, Texas

Damon L. Mitchell
Quality Auditor
Louisiana-Pacific Corporation
Conroe, Texas

Classroom Reviewers

Kathleen Avery
Teacher
Kellogg Science/Technology Magnet
Wichita, Kansas

Margaret S. Brown
Teacher
Cedar Grove Primary
Williamston, South Carolina

Deborah Browne
Teacher
Whitesville Elementary School
Moncks Corner, South Carolina

Wendy Capron
Teacher
Corlears School
New York, New York

Jiwon Choi
Teacher
Corlears School
New York, New York

John Cirrincione
Teacher
West Seneca Central Schools
West Seneca, New York

Jacqueline Colander
Teacher
Norfolk Public Schools
Norfolk, Virginia

Dr. Terry Contant
Teacher
Conroe Independent
School District
The Woodlands, Texas

Susan Crowley-Walsh
Teacher
Meadowbrook Elementary School
Gladstone, Missouri

Charlene K. Dindo
Teacher
Fairhope K-1 Center/Pelican's Nest
Science Lab
Fairhope, Alabama

Laurie Duffee
Teacher
Barnard Elementary
Tulsa, Oklahoma

Beth Anne Ebler
Teacher
Newark Public Schools
Newark, New Jersey

Karen P. Farrell
Teacher
Rondout Elementary School
District 72
Lake Forest, Illinois

Anna M. Gaiter
Teacher
Los Angeles Unified School District
Los Angeles Systemic Initiative
Los Angeles, California

Federica M. Gallegos
Teacher
Highland Park Elementary
Salt Lake School District
Salt Lake City, Utah

Janet E. Gray
Teacher
Anderson Elementary - Conroe ISD
Conroe, Texas

Karen Guinn
Teacher
Ehrhardt Elementary School - KISD
Spring, Texas

Denis John Hagerty
Teacher
Al Ittihad Private Schools
Dubai, United Arab Emirates

Judith Halpern
Teacher
Bannockburn School
Deerfield, Illinois

Debra D. Harper
Teacher
Community School District 9
Bronx, New York

Gretchen Harr
Teacher
Denver Public Schools - Doull School
Denver, Colorado

Bonnie L. Hawthorne
Teacher
Jim Darcy School
School District 1
Helena, Montana

Marselle Heywood-Julian
Teacher
Community School District 6
New York, New York

Scott Klene
Teacher
Bannockburn School 106
Bannockburn, Illinois

Thomas Kranz
Teacher
Livonia Primary School
Livonia, New York

Tom Leahy
Teacher
Coos Bay School District
Coos Bay, Oregon

Mary Littig
Teacher
Kellogg Science/Technology Magnet
Wichita, Kansas

Patricia Marin
Teacher
Corlears School
New York, New York

Susan Maki
Teacher
Cotton Creek CUSD 118
Island Lake, Illinois

Efraín Meléndez
Teacher
East LA Mathematics Science
Center LAUSD
Los Angeles, California

Becky Mojalid
Teacher
Manarat Jeddah Girls' School
Jeddah, Saudi Arabia

Susan Nations
Teacher
Sulphur Springs Elementary
Tampa, Florida

Brooke Palmer
Teacher
Whitesville Elementary
Moncks Corner, South Carolina

Jayne Pedersen
Teacher
Laura B. Sprague
School District 103
Lincolnshire, Illinois

Shirley Pfingston
Teacher
Orland School District 135
Orland Park, Illinois

Teresa Gayle Rountree
Teacher
Box Elder School District
Brigham City, Utah

Helen C. Smith
Teacher
Schultz Elementary
Klein Independent School District
Tomball, Texas

Denette Smith-Gibson
Teacher
Mitchell Intermediate, CISD
The Woodlands, Texas

Mary Jean Syrek
Teacher
Dr. Charles R. Drew Science
Magnet
Buffalo, New York

Rosemary Troxel
Teacher
Libertyville School District 70
Libertyville, Illinois

Susan D. Vani
Teacher
Laura B. Sprague School
School District 103
Lincolnshire, Illinois

Debra Worman
Teacher
Bryant Elementary
Tulsa, Oklahoma

Dr. Gayla Wright
Teacher
Edmond Public School
Edmond, Oklahoma

ISBN: 0-328-03447-9

Copyright © 2003, Pearson Education, Inc.
All Rights Reserved. Printed in the United States of America. This publication is protected by
Copyright, and permission should be obtained from the publisher prior to any prohibited
reproduction, storage in a retrieval system, or transmission in any form by any means, electronic,
mechanical, photocopying, recording, or likewise. For information regarding permission(s), write to:
Permissions Department, Scott Foresman, 1900 East Lake Avenue, Glenview, Illinois 60025.

3 4 5 6 7 8 9 10 V063 06 05 04 03

Activity and Safety Consultants

Laura Adams
Teacher
Holley-Navarre Intermediate
Navarre, Florida

Dr. Charlie Ashman
Teacher
Carl Sandburg Middle School
Mundelein District #75
Mundelein, Illinois

Christopher Atlee
Teacher
Horace Mann Elementary
Wichita Public Schools
Wichita, Kansas

David Bachman
Consultant
Chicago, Illinois

Sherry Baldwin
Teacher
Shady Brook
Bedford ISD
Euless, Texas

Pam Bazis
Teacher
Richardson ISD
  Classical Magnet School
Richardson, Texas

Angela Boese
Teacher
McCollom Elementary
Wichita Public Schools USD #259
Wichita, Kansas

Jan Buckelew
Teacher
Taylor Ranch Elementary
Venice, Florida

Shonie Castaneda
Teacher
Carman Elementary, PSJA
Pharr, Texas

Donna Coffey
Teacher
Melrose Elementary - Pinellas
St. Petersburg, Florida

Diamantina Contreras
Teacher
J.T. Brackenridge Elementary
San Antonio ISD
San Antonio, Texas

Susanna Curtis
Teacher
Lake Bluff Middle School
Lake Bluff, Illinois

Karen Farrell
Teacher
Rondout Elementary School,
  Dist. #72
Lake Forest, Illinois

Paul Gannon
Teacher
El Paso ISD
El Paso, Texas

Nancy Garman
Teacher
Jefferson Elementary School
Charleston, Illinois

Susan Graves
Teacher
Beech Elementary
Wichita Public Schools USD #259
Wichita, Kansas

Jo Anna Harrison
Teacher
Cornelius Elementary
Houston ISD
Houston, Texas

Monica Hartman
Teacher
Richard Elementary
Detroit Public Schools
Detroit, Michigan

Kelly Howard
Teacher
Sarasota, Florida

Kelly Kimborough
Teacher
Richardson ISD
  Classical Magnet School
Richardson, Texas

Mary Leveron
Teacher
Velasco Elementary
Brazosport ISD
Freeport, Texas

Becky McClendon
Teacher
A.P. Beutel Elementary
Brazosport ISD
Freeport, Texas

Suzanne Milstead
Teacher
Liestman Elementary
Alief ISD
Houston, Texas

Debbie Oliver
Teacher
School Board of Broward County
Ft. Lauderdale, Florida

Sharon Pearthree
Teacher
School Board of Broward County
Ft. Lauderdale, Florida

Jayne Pedersen
Teacher
Laura B. Sprague School
District 103
Lincolnshire, Illinois

Sharon Pedroja
Teacher
Riverside Cultural
  Arts/History Magnet
Wichita Public Schools USD #259
Wichita, Kansas

Marcia Percell
Teacher
Pharr, San Juan, Alamo ISD
Pharr, Texas

Shirley Pfingston
Teacher
Orland School Dist #135
Orland Park, Illinois

Sharon S. Placko
Teacher
District 26, Mt. Prospect
Mt. Prospect, IL

Glenda Rall
Teacher
Seltzer Elementary
USD #259
Wichita, Kansas

Nelda Requenez
Teacher
Canterbury Elementary
Edinburg, Texas

Dr. Beth Rice
Teacher
Loxahatchee Groves
  Elementary School
Loxahatchee, Florida

Martha Salom Romero
Teacher
El Paso ISD
El Paso, Texas

Paula Sanders
Teacher
Welleby Elementary School
Sunrise, Florida

Lynn Setchell
Teacher
Sigsbee Elementary School
Key West, Florida

Rhonda Shook
Teacher
Mueller Elementary
Wichita Public Schools USD #259
Wichita, Kansas

Anna Marie Smith
Teacher
Orland School Dist. #135
Orland Park, Illinois

Nancy Ann Varneke
Teacher
Seltzer Elementary
Wichita Public Schools USD #259
Wichita, Kansas

Aimee Walsh
Teacher
Rolling Meadows, Illinois

Ilene Wagner
Teacher
O.A. Thorp Scholastic Acacemy
Chicago Public Schools
Chicago, Illinois

Brian Warren
Teacher
Riley Community Consolidated
  School District 18
Marengo, Illinois

Tammie White
Teacher
Holley-Navarre
  Intermediate School
Navarre, Florida

Dr. Mychael Willon
Principal
Horace Mann Elementary
Wichita Public Schools
Wichita, Kansas

Inclusion Consultants

Dr. Eric J. Pyle, Ph.D.
Assistant Professor, Science Education
Department of Educational Theory
  and Practice
West Virginia University
Morgantown, West Virginia

Dr. Gretchen Butera, Ph.D.
Associate Professor, Special Education
Department of Education Theory
  and Practice
West Virginia University
Morgantown, West Virginia

Bilingual Consultant

Irma Gomez-Torres
Dalindo Elementary
Austin ISD
Austin, Texas

Bilingual Reviewers

Mary E. Morales
E.A. Jones Elementary
Fort Bend ISD
Missouri City, Texas

Gabriela T. Nolasco
Pebble Hills Elementary
Ysleta ISD
El Paso, Texas

Maribel B. Tanguma
Reed and Mock Elementary
San Juan, Texas

Yesenia Garza
Reed and Mock Elementary
San Juan, Texas

Teri Gallegos
St. Andrew's School
Austin, Texas

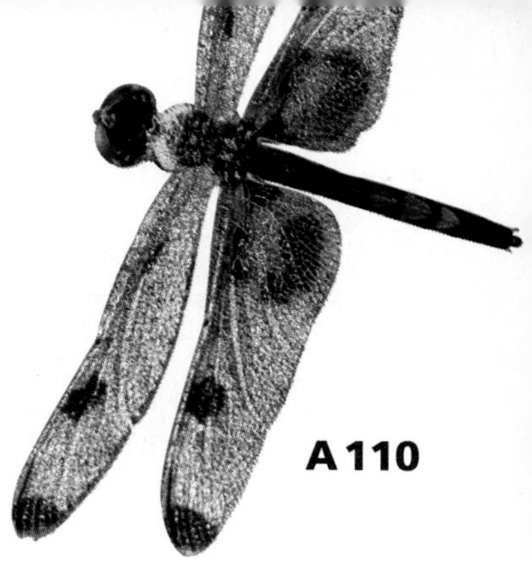

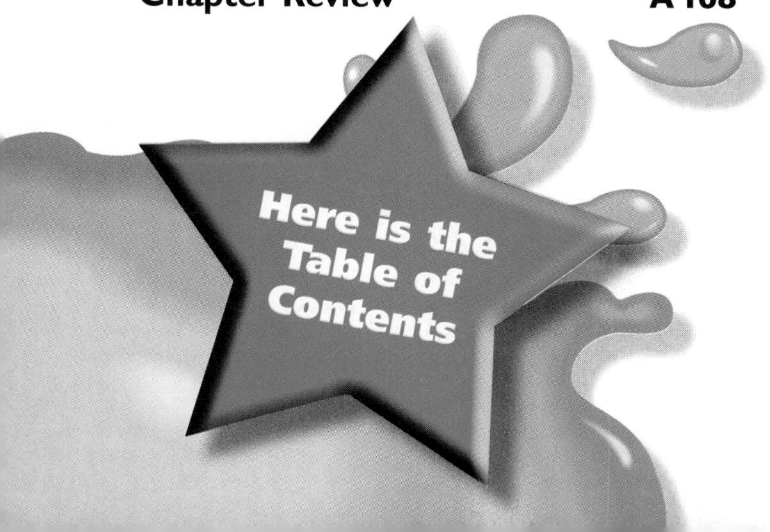

Here is the Table of Contents

Unit B
Physical Science

Go to LIFE SCIENCE UNIT A Table of Contents

Unit C
Earth Science

Go to LIFE SCIENCE UNIT A Table of Contents

Unit D
Human Body

Your Science Handbook

Go to LIFE SCIENCE UNIT A Table of Contents

Using Scientific Methods for Science Inquiry

Scientists try to solve many problems. Scientists study problems in different ways, but they all use scientific methods to guide their work. Scientific methods are organized ways of finding answers and solving problems. Scientific methods include the steps shown on these pages. The order of the steps or the number of steps used may change. You can use these steps to organize your own scientific inquiries.

State the Problem

The problem is the question you want to answer. Curiosity and inquiry have resulted in many scientific discoveries. State your problem in the form of a question.

Which sail design makes a boat move faster?

Formulate Your Hypothesis

Your hypothesis is a possible answer to your problem. Make sure your hypothesis can be tested. Your hypothesis should take the form of a statement.

◄ *A square sail will make a boat move faster.*

Identify and Control the Variables

For a fair test, you must select which variable to change and which variables to control. Choose one variable to change when you test your hypothesis. Control the other variables so they do not change.

▲ *Make one sail square and the other sail triangular. The other parts of the boat should be the same.*

Test Your Hypothesis

Do experiments to test your hypothesis. You may need to repeat experiments to make sure your results remain consistent. Sometimes you conduct a scientific survey to test a hypothesis.

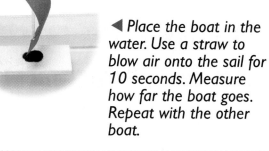

◀ Place the boat in the water. Use a straw to blow air onto the sail for 10 seconds. Measure how far the boat goes. Repeat with the other boat.

Collect Your Data

As you test your hypothesis, you will collect data about the problem you want to solve. You may need to record measurements. You might make drawings or diagrams. Or you may write lists or descriptions. Collect as much data as you can while testing your hypothesis.

Distance boat moved	
Square sail	43 cm
Triangular sail	26 cm

Interpret Your Data

By organizing your data into charts, tables, diagrams, and graphs, you may see patterns in the data. Then you can decide what the information from your data means.

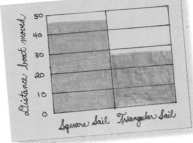

State Your Conclusion

Your conclusion is a decision you make based on evidence. Compare your results with your hypothesis. Based on whether or not your data supports your hypothesis, decide if your hypothesis is correct or incorrect. Then communicate your conclusion by stating or presenting your decision.

The square sail moves the boat faster.

? Inquire Further

Use what you learn to solve other problems or to answer other questions that you might have. You may decide to repeat your experiment, or to change it based on what you learned.

◀ Does the shape of the boat affect its speed?

Using Process Skills for Science Inquiry

These 12 process skills are used by scientists when they do their research. You also use many of these skills every day. For example, when you think of a statement that you can test, you are using process skills. When you gather data to make a chart or graph, you are using process skills. As you do the activities in your book, you will use these same process skills.

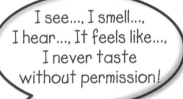

I see..., I smell..., I hear..., It feels like..., I never taste without permission!

Observing

Use one or more of your senses—seeing, hearing, smelling, touching, or tasting—to gather information about objects or events.

	High	Low	Precipitation
Atlanta	73	54	.04
Austin	76	57	—
Los Angeles	54	41	.01
New York City	52	46	—
Orlando	83	62	—

Communicating

Share information about what you learn using words, pictures, charts, graphs, and diagrams.

Classifying

Arrange or group objects according to their common properties.

◀ *Shells with one color in Group 1.*

Shells with two or more colors in Group 2. ▶

Estimating and Measuring

Make an estimate about an object's properties, then measure and describe the object in units.

I think what's in here is shaped like . . .

Inferring

Draw a conclusion or make a reasonable guess based on what you observe, or from your past experiences.

Predicting

Form an idea about what will happen based on evidence.

◀ *Predict what type of sail will work best.*

Making Operational Definitions

Define or describe an object or event based on your experiences with it.

An acid is a substance that changes blue litmus paper to... ▶

Making and Using Models

Make real or mental representations to explain ideas, objects, or events.

◀ *My model mouth is like a real mouth because...*

Formulating Questions and Hypotheses

Think of a statement that you can test to solve a problem or to answer a question about how something works.

If I add another washer... ▶

Collecting and Interpreting Data

Gather observations and measurements into graphs, tables, charts, or diagrams. Then use the information to solve problems or answer questions.

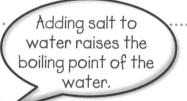

Adding salt to water raises the boiling point of the water.

Identifying and Controlling Variables

Change one factor that may affect the outcome of an event while holding other factors constant.

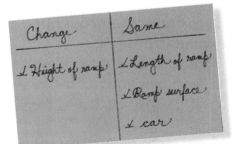

Change	Same
∠ Height of ramp	∠ Length of ramp
	∠ Ramp surface
	∠ car

Experimenting

Design an investigation to test a hypothesis or to solve a problem. Then form a conclusion.

I'll write a clear procedure so that other students could repeat the experiment.

Science Inquiry

Throughout your science book, you will ask questions, do investigations, answer your questions, and tell others what you have learned. Use the descriptions below to help you during your scientific inquiries.

1 Ask questions that can be answered by scientific investigations.
Direct your questions and inquiries toward objects and events that can be described, explained, or predicted by scientific investigations.

2 Design and conduct a scientific investigation.
Investigations can include using scientific methods to carry out science inquiry. As you conduct your investigations, you will relate your ideas to current scientific knowledge, suggest alternate explanations, and evaluate explanations and procedures.

3 Use appropriate tools, and methods to gather, analyze, and interpret data.
The tools and methods you use will depend on the questions you ask and the investigations you design. A computer can be a useful tool for collecting, summarizing, and displaying your data.

4 Use data to develop descriptions, suggest explanations, make predictions, and construct models.
Base your explanations and descriptions on the information that you have gathered. In addition, understanding scientific subject matter will help you develop explanations, identify causes, and recognize relationships of events you observe with science content.

5 Use logic to make relationships between data and explanations.
Review and summarize the data you have gathered in your investigation. Use logic to determine the cause and effect relationships in the events and variables you observe.

6 Analyze alternative explanations and predictions.
Listen to, consider, and evaluate explanations offered by others. Asking questions and querying and evaluating explanations is part of scientific inquiry.

7 Communicate procedures and explanations.
Share your investigations with others by describing your methods, observations, results, and explanations.

8 Use mathematics to analyze data and construct explanations.
Use mathematics in your investigations to gather, organize, and collect data and to present explanations and results in a meaningful manner.

Unit A
Life Science

Science and Technology
In Your World!

Artificial Skin Has Burn Injuries Covered

Scientists make artificial skin using molecules from body parts from cows. When the artificial skin is placed over the injured skin, natural skin cells grow back with little scarring. Learn about cells that make up living things in **Chapter 1 Structure and Function of Cells.**

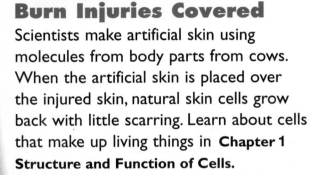

Making Plants that Insects Hate

In the never-ending battle against insects and diseases that destroy corn, potatoes, apples, and many other food crops, scientists have a powerful weapon—genes. Changing a plant's genes can make it tasty to us, but untasty to bugs. Learn more about genes and traits in **Chapter 2 Reproduction and Heredity.**

Satellites Spot Fossils from Space

How can satellites "see" fossils from space? Devices that detect heat and moisture content point scientists to rocks where fossils are likely to be found. Learn more about fossils in **Chapter 3 Changing and Adapting.**

A Glimpse of Tomorrow

What will happen to plants as pollution increases? To find out, scientists pump carbon dioxide and other gases onto test fields. By mimicking air as it might be in the future, they hope to discover pollution's effect on plant life. Learn more about the environment in **Chapter 4 Ecosystems and Biomes.**

Brrrripp! Hello!!

IT'S ALIVE! It's green, shiny, smooth, and cool to touch! Say, is it a plant—or an animal? **WHOOPS!** This one jumps! When you get right down to it, what **ARE** the differences between plants and animals?

Chapter 1
Structure and Function of Cells

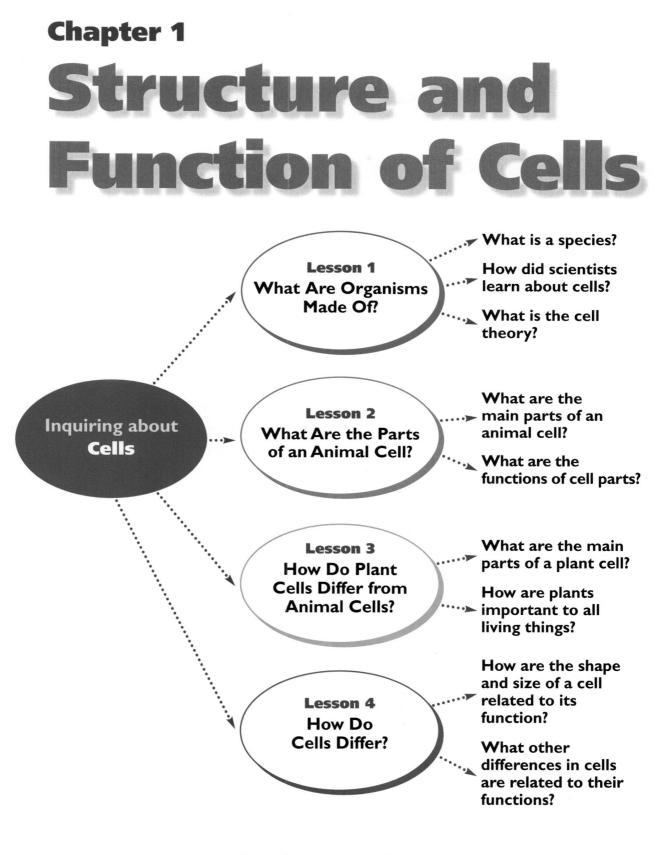

Inquiring about Cells

Lesson 1
What Are Organisms Made Of?
- What is a species?
- How did scientists learn about cells?
- What is the cell theory?

Lesson 2
What Are the Parts of an Animal Cell?
- What are the main parts of an animal cell?
- What are the functions of cell parts?

Lesson 3
How Do Plant Cells Differ from Animal Cells?
- What are the main parts of a plant cell?
- How are plants important to all living things?

Lesson 4
How Do Cells Differ?
- How are the shape and size of a cell related to its function?
- What other differences in cells are related to their functions?

Copy the chapter graphic organizer onto your own paper. This organizer shows you what the whole chapter is all about. As you read the lessons and do the activities, look for answers to the questions and write them on your organizer.

Exploring Magnification

Process Skills
- predicting
- observing
- inferring
- communicating

Materials
- safety goggles
- wire
- sharpened pencil
- newspaper
- cup of water

Explore

1. Put on your safety goggles.

2. Straighten a 10 cm piece of thin wire. Make a loop in the end of the wire by winding it around the sharpened end of a pencil. Your loop should be 5 mm across.

3. Place the loop into a cup of water. Slowly pull the loop out of the water. There should be a water drop in the loop. If not, dip the loop into the water again.

4. What will happen if you view newspaper through the water-filled loop? Record your **prediction.** Explain a past experience that led you to make your prediction.

5. Test your prediction by holding the water drop over a section of newspaper. Move the loop toward and away from the newspaper until you can see the print clearly. Record what you **observe** through the loop.

6. Move the loop away from the newsprint and blow out the water drop. Place the empty loop over the same letters in the newsprint as in step 5. Record what you see through the loop.

Reflect

What can you **infer** from your prediction and observations? **Communicate** your ideas with others in the group. Make a list of the ways that magnification can help you study living things.

? Inquire Further

What would the newsprint look like if you viewed it through another substance, such as oil? Develop a plan to answer this or other questions you may have.

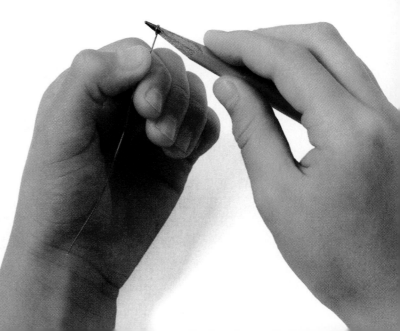

Bar Graphs

The adult human body is made up of trillions of cells, such as blood cells, brain cells, and skin cells. Each type of cell has different characteristics and a different function.

You can use **bar graphs** to organize and compare data about cells or other topics.

Math Vocabulary

bar graph, a graph using horizontal or vertical bars to display numerical information

Example

This bar graph shows approximately how long different kinds of blood cells live. How much longer than a platelet does a red blood cell live?

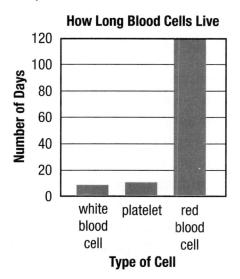

How Long Blood Cells Live

Did you know?

The color of blood varies among animals. All vertebrates have red blood. Segmented worms have blood that is green or red. Some crustaceans, which includes shrimp and lobsters, have blue blood!

Look at the bar for the platelet. It represents 10 days. The red blood cell bar represents 120 days. So, since 120 - 10 = 110, red blood cells live 110 days longer than platelets.

Talk About It!

How does a bar graph show the value of a data item?

You will learn:
- what a species is.
- how scientists learned about cells.
- what the cell theory is.

Glossary

Glossary

species (spē′shēz), a group of organisms that have the same characteristics and are able to produce offspring that can reproduce

▲ *Life exists in a small area above and below the surface of the earth. Some microscopic organisms live in the almost freezing cold of the upper atmosphere. Some of the many different kinds of organisms can be seen on the next page.*

Lesson 1

What Are Organisms Made Of?

It's **big** and **green**—and it's **moving!** Should you be afraid of this living creature? Not unless you have a fear of pine trees blowing in the wind! Organisms come in many sizes, shapes, and colors. How else do living creatures differ? How are they the same?

Earth's Species

All the organisms you see pictured on the next page live on Earth. Some live on land or underground. Others live in the air. Still others live in water. Organisms can live only where they can get the things they need.

Most life is found only in a small layer of the earth, from just below the surface to the lower part of the atmosphere. Imagine that you could shrink the earth so that it was the size of an apple. As you can see at the left, the layer where living things are found would be thin like the peel of that apple. Yet within that thin layer, numerous kinds of life exist. In fact, more than 30 million different kinds of living things live on Earth. Each different kind of organism is a **species.** What's so special about species? Just how do scientists tell them apart?

Individuals in a species share certain characteristics. For example, all humans belong to a single species. What characteristics do they share?

Only members of the same species can mate and produce offspring that, in turn, can mate and produce offspring. That is, monarch butterflies produce monarch butterflies that can produce more monarch butterflies.

Not only is there an amazing number of species on Earth, but there is an amazing variety among them. Yet no matter how different organisms are from one another, they all have one thing in common. All organisms are made of cells.

Variations Among Living Things

Just one look at the species pictured here shows you how they can differ in size and complexity.

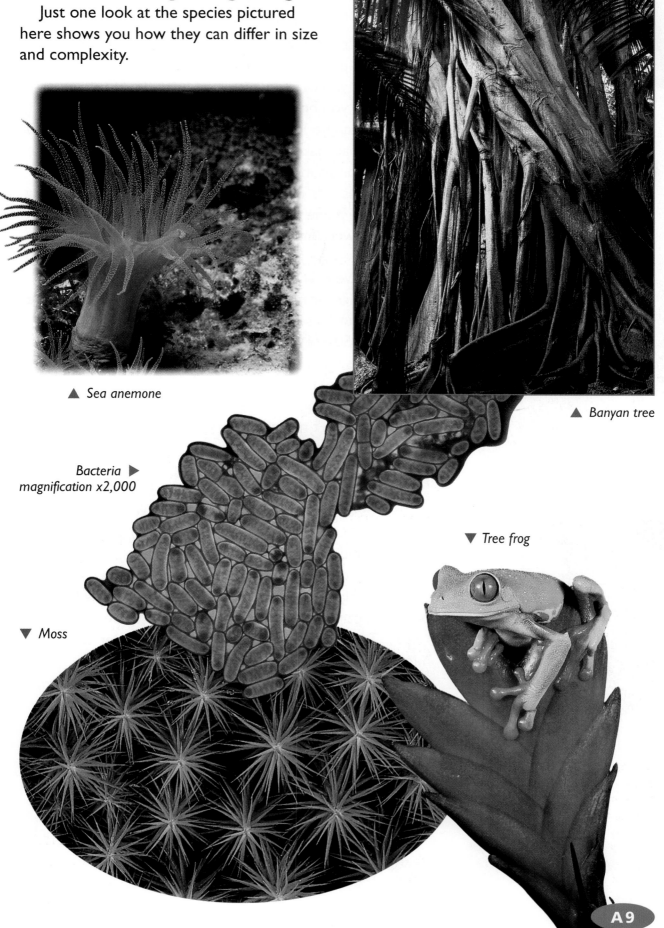

▲ Sea anemone

▲ Banyan tree

Bacteria ▶
magnification x2,000

▼ Tree frog

▼ Moss

Glossary

compound microscope
(kom′pound mī′krə skōp), microscope having more than one lens

Robert Hooke's microscope allowed him to see the tiny compartments, or cells, in a piece of cork. He made detailed sketches, such as this one, to record what he saw. ▼

Discovery of Cells

History of Science

If you hold your arm out and look at the palm and fingers of your hand, you can see patterns of lines. Move your hand closer, and you can see even more details. However, if you bring your hand too close to your face, your eyes can no longer focus. Your hand appears blurred. The cells that make up the skin on your hand are simply too small for your eyes to see.

For thousands of years, scientists wondered what living things were made of. However, like you trying to see your hand, they were limited by their eyes and could not see tiny details.

If you have ever used a hand lens, you know that the lens magnifies, or makes larger, what you see. People have known about lenses for almost two thousand years. About A.D. 50, they were using lenses—as toys! Around 1300, lenses were made to correct vision problems—the first eyeglasses. By the mid-1400s, scientists were using lenses to study extremely small things. However, a single lens just couldn't magnify a very tiny object enough for scientists to learn much.

Finally, around 1590, a Dutch eyeglass maker, Hans Janssen, and his son, Zacharias, put two lenses together at the opposite ends of a tube. They had invented the first **compound microscope.**

In the mid-1600s, the English scientist Robert Hooke used the compound microscope you see in the picture to peer at a thin slice of cork. He saw "a great many little boxes" separated by walls. Hooke called these little boxes "cells." Today we still use the term *cells* to refer to the microscopic building blocks of all living things.

Above the microscope, you can see what Hooke saw when he looked under the microscope. The cork that he looked at did not contain living cells. Rather, Hooke saw the cell walls that had surrounded cork cells when they were living. The other important materials that were the basis of life were missing.

Living organisms were studied by Dutch lens grinder, Anton van Leeuwenhoek. Around 1673, he used a simple microscope to look at a drop of water. He called the tiny organisms he observed "wee beasties." Leeuwenhoek also used a microscope to study teeth scrapings and blood cells.

Although these early scientists saw things that no one had ever seen before, their microscopes actually did not provide very good images. Their lenses were made of poor-quality glass. Today's microscopes are very different from those used by Hooke and Leeuwenhoek. For example, Hooke's microscope was able to magnify objects only 30 times. Today's best compound microscopes can magnify objects more than 1,500 times. You can see the parts of a compound microscope below.

Typical Compound Microscope

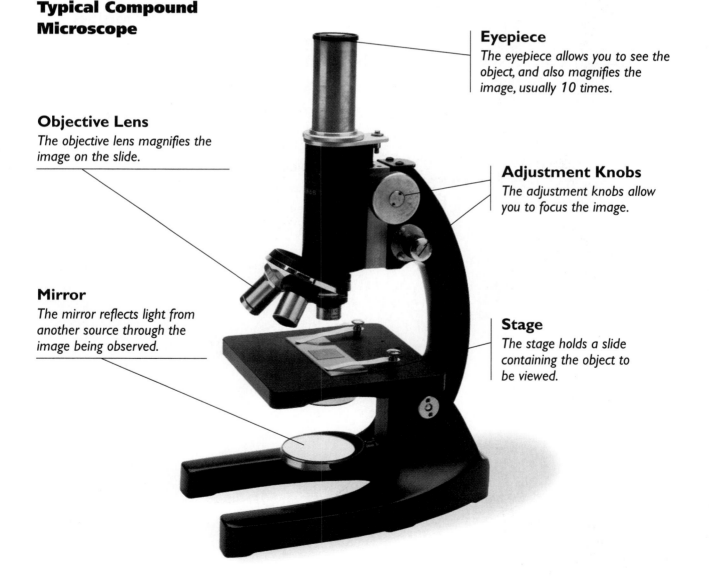

Objective Lens
The objective lens magnifies the image on the slide.

Mirror
The mirror reflects light from another source through the image being observed.

Eyepiece
The eyepiece allows you to see the object, and also magnifies the image, usually 10 times.

Adjustment Knobs
The adjustment knobs allow you to focus the image.

Stage
The stage holds a slide containing the object to be viewed.

Light Microscope

If you looked at a feather under a compound microscope, you might see something like this. ▼

A compound microscope is a light microscope. You place the object to be viewed on a glass slide and position the slide on the microscope stage over a small opening. This stage opening allows light from a mirror or lamp to shine through the object to be viewed. The light then passes through magnifying lenses.

Light microscopes can magnify objects many times their actual size. However, at times this magnification is not enough. Very tiny structures that are close together appear blurred.

 Physical Science

Today, scientists can use electron microscopes, similar to the one below, to study "wee beasties" and to look directly into cells. Instead of light, an electron microscope uses beams of atomic particles called electrons to produce an image. You can then see the magnified image on a screen or photographic plate.

Electron microscopes produce sharper pictures than do light microscopes. They can clearly magnify objects up to one million times. Look how different feathers appear when they are viewed with a light microscope and an electron microscope.

Electron Microscope

▲ *Magnified 270 times under an electron microscope, a feather appears like this.*

Electron microscopes use electrons to make things look up to one million times bigger. They allow scientists to study cells in great detail. ▶

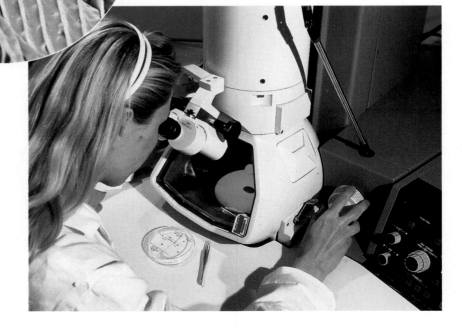

Cell Theory

History of Science

Although Robert Hooke discovered cells in the mid-1600s, it took nearly 200 years for scientists to understand just what they were. Even after Hooke's discovery, many scientists thought that life could develop from nonliving matter. For example, around 1600, a Belgian doctor placed wheat grains in a sweaty shirt. He placed the shirt on the floor in the corner of a room. When he returned several weeks later, he found mice. The doctor concluded that human sweat changed wheat grains to mice. Later scientists conducted experiments that proved this idea wrong.

As the years went by, scientists made more and more observations of microscopic organisms. They began to realize that cells are the building blocks of all living things. In the 1800s, three German biologists—Theodor Schwann, Matthias Schleiden, and Rudolph Virchow—developed the **cell theory**. This theory states the following:

• The cell is the basic unit of all living organisms.
• Only living cells can produce new living cells.

The cell theory points out the basic similarity among very different organisms—they are all made of cells. You can see by the pictures on this page that some organisms, such as the meerkat, are made of many cells, while others, like the green alga, are made of only one.

Meerkats are many-celled animals that live in parts of Africa. ▶

Glossary

cell theory
(sel thē/ər ē), theory stating that the cell is the basic unit of all living organisms, and only living cells can produce new living cells

Some organisms, such as this green alga, are made of a single cell. Green algae produce their own food. ▼

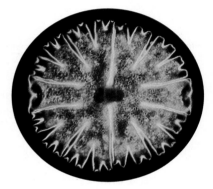

magnification x170

Lesson 1 Review

1. What is a species?
2. How did scientists learn about cells?
3. What is the cell theory?
4. **Bar Graphs**
   Species vary in life span. Make a bar graph, in years, of the maximum life spans of these animals: goldfish, 41; giant panda, 26; platypus, 17; cat, 34.

Investigating Cells

Process Skills

- observing
- communicating
- classifying

Materials

- microscope
- prepared slide of animal cells
- scissors
- elodea plant
- forceps
- microscope slide with coverslip
- dropper
- cup of water

Getting Ready

In this activity you'll find out how plant and animal cells are alike and how they are different.

Follow This Procedure

1 Make a chart like the one shown. Use your chart to record your observations.

Animal Cells	Elodea

2 Place a microscope on the table in front of you (Photo A). Study each part of the microscope to find out what it does. Find the light source, the eyepiece, and the objective lens.

3 Locate the adjustment knob that moves the stage closer or farther from the objective lens. Turn the adjustment knob so that the lens is almost touching the stage.

4 Place a prepared microscope slide of animal cells on the stage of the microscope. Look through the eyepiece. Use the adjustment knob to move the lens away from the microscope slide until you can clearly see the animal cells. Fine-tune your adjustment.

5 **Observe** the animal cells. Find the cytoplasm, cell membrane, and nucleus. Make a drawing to **communicate** what you see.

Self-Monitoring

Have I drawn all the cell parts that I can see?

Photo A

Photo B

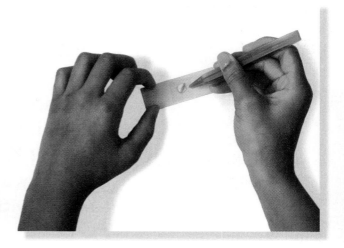

Photo C

⑥ Use the scissors to remove a leaf tip from an elodea plant (Photo B).

⑦ Use forceps to place the leaf tip on a microscope slide. Use a dropper to add a drop of water to the slide. Then use the forceps to carefully cover the leaf with a coverslip (Photo C).

⑧ Place the slide on the microscope stage. Observe the leaf through the microscope. Draw what you see.

Interpret Your Results

1. Look at your drawings of the plant and animal cells. Explain how the plant and animal cells that you observed are alike and different.

2. Tell what characteristics you could use to **classify** a cell as either a plant or an animal cell.

 **Inquire Further**

Do all plant cells have the same parts? Develop a plan to answer this or other questions you may have.

Self-Assessment

- I followed instructions to **observe** plant and animal cells.
- I identified the parts of plant and animal cells.
- I **communicated** by drawing my observations.
- I compared and contrasted plant and animal cells.
- I used cell characteristics as a way to **classify** plant and animal cells.

What Are the Parts of an Animal Cell?

What's the Big Idea?

You will learn:

- what the main parts of an animal cell are.
- what the functions are of some cell parts.

Walls, a ceiling, and a floor surround your school. What **inside** parts make up your school? You might answer, "The classrooms, a library, and a gym." Would the space be a school without these parts?

Glossary

nucleus (nü′klē əs), part of the cell that controls activities of other cell parts

chromosome (kro′mə sōm), stringlike structure in a cell nucleus that carries information controlling all the cell's activities

In this electron microscopic image of a liver cell, you can easily see the nucleus. ▼

Animal Cells

Just as your school wouldn't be a school without the parts inside it, neither would a cell. All cells have important parts that have certain functions.

A cell is like a school with many rooms. A school usually has offices, a gym, a cafeteria, a boiler room, a library, and classrooms. Having separate rooms allows different activities to be carried out in particular places.

Most cells have the same basic structure. The photo to the left shows part of an animal cell as it might be seen under an electron microscope. The first thing you probably notice is the **nucleus**. The nucleus is the control center of the cell. It is like the main office in a school.

Inside the nucleus is a stringlike structure called a **chromosome**. Chromosomes store directions that the cell uses to carry on activities. They control processes such as how fast a cell grows or when it reproduces.

Not all organisms have the same number of chromosomes in their cells. You—and all other normal humans— have 46 chromosomes in each body cell. A housefly has 12 chromosomes in each of its body cells, a cat has 38, a dog has 78, and a crayfish has 200.

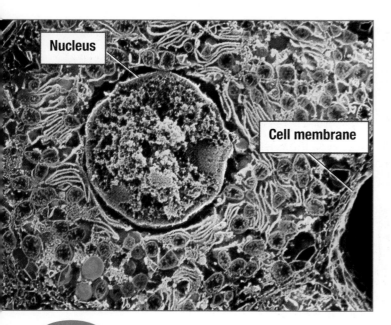

Nucleus

Cell membrane

Just as walls, ceilings, and floors hold a school building together, a **cell membrane** holds the contents of a cell together. It gives support and shape to the cell. This thin, flexible covering helps the cell by allowing only certain substances to enter or leave it.

Think of people who stand by the doors of a school to control who enters or leaves the building. Like the monitors, the cell membrane controls what comes into and goes out of the cell. You can see in the picture below that the cell membrane allows materials such as oxygen to enter the cell. These substances are needed by the cell for energy and growth. The cell membrane also allows wastes such as carbon dioxide to leave the cell. The membrane also protects the cell by keeping substances that could harm the cell outside.

Cytoplasm fills the space inside the cell between the cell membrane and the nucleus. **Cytoplasm** is a clear, jellylike material similar to the white of a raw egg. It is made mostly of water. Cells depend on water for their survival. Without water, cells could not carry out all their necessary activities. Your body cells are more than two-thirds water. That's why you could not survive more than about four days without water.

Glossary

cell membrane
(sel mem′brān), thin outer covering that holds a cell together

cytoplasm
(sī′tə plaz′əm), clear, jellylike material that fills the space between the cell membrane and the nucleus

Oxygen and carbon dioxide can move through the cell membrane. ▼

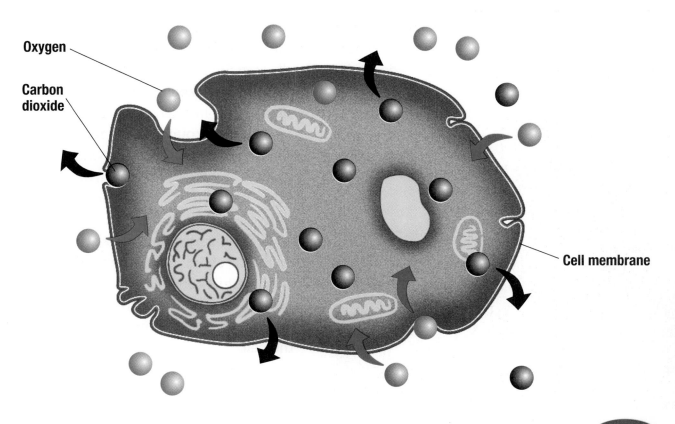

Oxygen

Carbon dioxide

Cell membrane

Glossary

organelle (ôr′gə nel′), tiny structure in the cytoplasm of a cell that performs a special job

mitochondria (mī′tə kon′drē ə), organelles where food and oxygen react to release energy

vacuole (vak′yü ōl), saclike organelle used for storing materials

endoplasmic reticulum (en′dō plaz′mik ri tik′yə ləm), organelle that transports materials inside the cell

ribosome (rī′bə sōm), organelle that puts together proteins for the cell

These ball-shaped cells store fats. Fats not used in the body are carried to these cells through tiny blood vessels, which you can see in blue. ▼

Functions of Cell Parts

Inside the cytoplasm of all cells, including the fat cells below, are tiny parts that have special jobs. Each of these structures is an **organelle**. Just as each kind of room in a school has a different function, so does each organelle in a cell. You can see some of these organelles in the diagram on the next page.

Think about what happens in a school boiler room. Fuel is burned to make heat energy. Likewise, scattered throughout a cell's cytoplasm are **mitochondria**. Food and oxygen react in these bean-shaped organelles to release energy. This energy is needed to run the cells. Mitochondria are the "powerhouses" of cells. A cell can have as few as one mitochondrion or as many as 10,000 mitochondria or more. The number depends on the cell's level of activity. The more active a cell is, the more energy it needs and the more mitochondria it has.

Where does a school store the supplies it needs? Many schools store these materials in closets and storage rooms. Where do they store wastepaper and other trash until it can be disposed of? A school stores them in wastebaskets and dumpsters, of course.

Cells also need storage spaces. A **vacuole** is an organelle that stores nutrients and water, as well as waste products. Materials pass into and out of vacuoles through a thin membrane. Some vacuoles can expand and contract as needed. Animal cells contain many small vacuoles.

You and your fellow students need to be able to move from one classroom to another in a school. Books and supplies also need to be moved around. In a school, the hallways serve this purpose.

Cells also need to move materials from one part to another. The organelle that handles this function looks like a series of channels. It is called the **endoplasmic reticulum**, or ER for short. Some parts of the endoplasmic reticulum are covered by tiny structures called **ribosomes**. Ribosomes put together proteins for the cell.

magnification x1038

Look at the typical animal cell below. Nearly all animal cells have a cell membrane, cytoplasm, and a nucleus with chromosomes, but the number of chromosomes in the nucleus varies from species to species. (That's what helps make each species unique.) Also, the number of each kind of organelle varies among the cells of different kinds of organisms. The number also varies among different cells in the same organism.

Typical Animal Cell

Vacuole
Vacuoles store water, nutrients, and wastes.

Endoplasmic Reticulum
The endoplasmic reticulum moves materials throughout the cell.

Nucleus
The nucleus is the control center of the cell.

Mitochondrion
Mitochondria release the energy stored in food.

Ribosome
Ribosomes produce proteins for the cell.

Cell Membrane
The cell membrane holds the parts of the cell together and controls the movement of materials into and out of the cell.

Cytoplasm
Cytoplasm fills most of the cell outside the nucleus. Organelles float in the cytoplasm.

Lesson 2 Review

1. What are the main parts of an animal cell?

2. Name three organelles in an animal cell and tell what each does.

3. **Bar Graphs**
   Make a bar graph showing the number of chromosomes in the cells of humans, dogs, houseflies, and crayfish.

How Do Plant Cells Differ from Animal Cells?

What's the Big Idea?

You will learn:

- what the parts of a plant cell are.
- how plants are important to all living things.

Glossary

chloroplast
(klôr′ə plast), organelle that makes sugars, using carbon dioxide, water, and the energy from sunlight

chlorophyll (klôr′ə fil), green substance in the chloroplasts that traps energy from sunlight

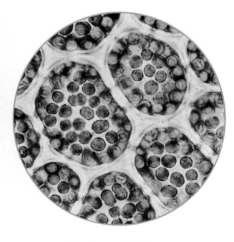

The chloroplasts in these moss cells contain chlorophyll. The chloroplasts enable the plant to make glucose. ▼

magnification x1100

Ahh! Sit outside in the sunlight all day. Take in some air, water, and minerals. What if that's all you needed to do to survive? Sound hard to believe? You can't do it, but a plant can. That's because its cells have special parts that your cells don't.

Plant Cells

Nearly all animal and plant cells contain cell membranes, nuclei, cytoplasm, and other organelles, but they differ in some ways too. First, plant cells are usually much larger than animal cells. Second, plant cells usually have only one large vacuole. Animal cells often have many smaller ones.

Look at the diagram of the plant cell on the next page. The large vacuole of a plant cell is located near the center of the cell. It fills with water and pushes the cytoplasm against the cell membrane. That pressure helps to keep the cell firm.

If you have ever noticed a wilting plant, you have seen a plant whose cells are low in water. The vacuoles have shrunk, so the plant's cells have become less stiff. Give the plant water, and the vacuoles in its cells will fill with water and make the plant firm again. Animal cells shrink too when there isn't enough water, but not as much as plant cells do.

Perhaps the most important way that plant cells and animal cells differ is that many plant cells have organelles called **chloroplasts.** You can see these green, egg-shaped organelles scattered in the cytoplasm of the plant cells at the left. Inside each chloroplast is a green substance called **chlorophyll.** Chlorophyll traps energy from the sun to make sugars. Animal cells can't do that.

If you live in a region where leaves change color in the fall, you have seen the presence—and disappearance—of chlorophyll in chloroplasts. Chloroplasts belong to a group of organelles called plastids. Plastids store plants' colors—green, red, orange, yellow, or blue. Normally, the green of chlorophyll hides the other colors in the chloroplasts. In fall, when temperatures drop, chlorophyll breaks down, and other colors in the leaf show through.

A plant cell has a **cell wall** in addition to a cell membrane. The tough, nonliving material of the wall acts like an outer skeleton for each cell. It gives the cell support, strength, and shape. In Lesson 1, you read about Robert Hooke and his famous discovery. It was the cell walls of cork that Hooke saw under the microscope. The living material that had been inside the walls of the cork tree cells was no longer there.

cell wall (sel wôl), tough, nonliving material that acts like an outside skeleton for each plant cell

Typical Plant Cell

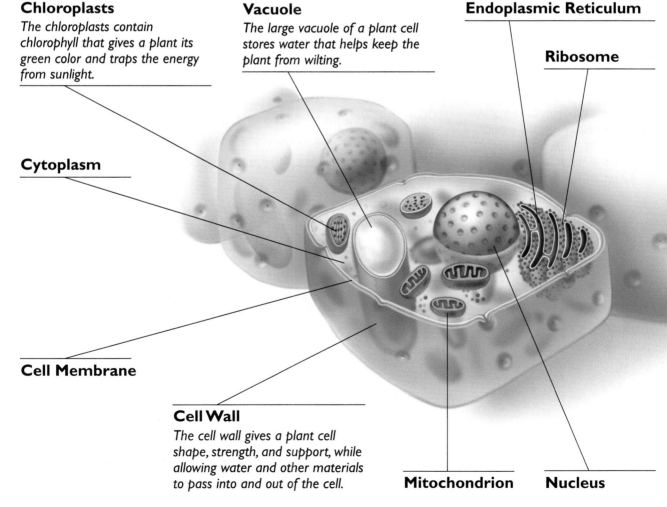

Chloroplasts
The chloroplasts contain chlorophyll that gives a plant its green color and traps the energy from sunlight.

Vacuole
The large vacuole of a plant cell stores water that helps keep the plant from wilting.

Endoplasmic Reticulum

Ribosome

Cytoplasm

Cell Membrane

Cell Wall
The cell wall gives a plant cell shape, strength, and support, while allowing water and other materials to pass into and out of the cell.

Mitochondrion

Nucleus

Importance of Plants

The sun showers Earth with huge amounts of energy in the form of sunlight. Most of this energy is absorbed by the land or the oceans, or it is reflected back into space. However, a small percentage of this energy is absorbed by green plants, such as the bean plant below.

Then a complex and important process takes place. In fact, it is a process on which you and almost all life on Earth depend. The chlorophyll in green plant cells traps the energy from the sun. The chloroplast also uses carbon dioxide that the plant takes in from the air and water that is transported through plant roots and stems. With these three ingredients, the chloroplast makes glucose, a simple sugar, during a process called photosynthesis. *Photo* means "light," and *synthesis* means "putting together." So *photosynthesis* means "putting together with light." During photosynthesis, oxygen is also formed and released by the plant into the atmosphere.

What a plant can do, then, is change light energy into chemical energy, which is stored in glucose. This chemical energy is stored until the plant needs it to grow, transport materials, or perform some other process.

What happens when a plant needs some of this energy? Remember that the mitochondria are the powerhouses of a cell. When a plant needs energy, a process called respiration occurs in its cells' mitochondria. Oxygen is used in a process that releases the energy stored in the glucose.

The energy for photosynthesis comes from sunlight. Green plants use it to combine carbon dioxide and water to make simple sugars. Oxygen is given off during photosynthesis. ▼

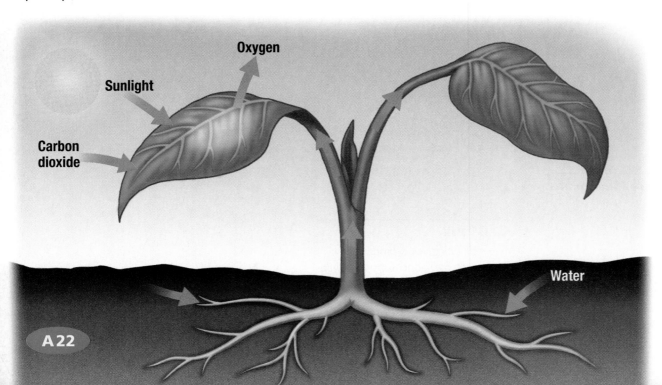

Oxygen

Sunlight

Carbon dioxide

Water

Carbon dioxide and water are produced during this process. How is respiration different from photosynthesis?

If you need food, you can't just sit in the sun for a few hours while drinking water and taking in carbon dioxide. Neither can any other animal. The reason is simple. Neither you nor other animals have cells that contain chlorophyll. Animals, unlike plants, can't make their own food. Then how do animals get the energy they need? They get it from eating food. They get food energy when they eat plants or when they eat other organisms that have eaten plants.

For example, the caterpillar in the picture is munching hungrily on a leaf. Some of the energy it gets from the leaf will be stored in its body. Then along comes the bird pictured below, who likes a fat, juicy caterpillar for a meal. That bird gets its food energy when it eats and digests the caterpillar that has eaten the plant.

What about the peanut-butter-and-jelly sandwich and glass of milk you have after school? Where did this food come from? The peanut butter is made from seeds of the peanut plant. Grape jelly is made from grapes—the fruit of another plant. The bread is made with flour from wheat seeds—still another plant. The milk comes from a cow. However, before the cow could produce milk, it needed the energy it got from eating grass.

▲ How is this leaf a source of energy for these caterpillars?

Some animals get energy from eating other animals. This bird gets energy from eating the caterpillar. ▼

Lesson 3 Review

1. How do plant cells differ from animal cells?

2. How are plants important to all living things?

3. **Bar Graphs**
   Using the diagrams on pages A19 and A21, make a bar graph comparing the parts of a plant cell and an animal cell.

Investigating Pigments

Process Skills

- observing
- predicting
- communicating
- making operational definitions

Materials

- safety goggles
- parsley
- 6 plastic cups
- scissors
- dropper
- rubbing alcohol
- 3 spoons
- 3 flat toothpicks
- 3 filter paper strips
- tape
- 3 pencils
- mushrooms
- beet leaves
- paper towel

Getting Ready

How do the pigments in parsley, beet leaves, and mushrooms differ? In this activity you will separate the pigments in these organisms.

Follow This Procedure

1 Make a chart like the one shown. Use your chart to record your predictions and observations.

Test material	Color of liquid	Predictions	Observations
Parsley			
Mushrooms			
Beet leaves			

2 Put on your safety goggles. Place several parsley leaves in a plastic cup. Use scissors to cut the leaves into very small pieces. Add 2–3 droppersful of rubbing alcohol. Crush the leaves in the alcohol with the back of a spoon. **Observe** and record the color of the alcohol solution.

3 Use a toothpick to place a small drop of the parsley liquid about 0.5 cm from the bottom of a filter paper strip (Photo A). When the drop is dry, place a second drop of the parsley liquid on top of the first. Do the same for two more drops.

4 Label the strip with the letter *P*. Tape it to a pencil.

5 Repeat steps 2–4 with the mushrooms and with the beet leaves, labeling the strips *M* and *B*.

6 Fill 3 plastic cups with about 1 cm of rubbing alcohol.

Photo A

Photo B

7 Place one pencil across the top of each cup of alcohol so that the bottom of the paper strip is just touching the alcohol (Photo B). Be sure that the drops you placed on the strip are not touching the alcohol.

8 As the alcohol rises up the strip, you will be able to see the different pigments that give the test item its color. **Predict** what colors you will see. On what information did you base your predictions?

9 Allow the alcohol to rise up the paper to a height of 7 cm. Remove the strips from the alcohol and lay them on a paper towel to dry. Observe the filter strips. Record your observations in your chart.

Interpret Your Results

1. Did the color of the alcohol solutions always match the color shown on the filter paper? Based on the results of this activity, which test items can you conclude contain more than one pigment?

2. How is the mushroom strip different?

3. How could you use this activity to tell whether a test item was a plant? **Communicate** your ideas to the group.

4. An **operational definition** describes what an object does, or what you can observe about the object. Write an operational definition of a green plant leaf.

Inquire Further

What pigments might you find in the leaves, roots, and stems of a carrot plant? Develop a plan to answer this or other questions you may have.

Self-Assessment

- I followed instructions to separate pigments in test organisms.
- I **predicted** what pigments would be present in each test item.
- I recorded my **observations** about the colors that appeared on the filter paper.
- I **communicated** how to tell whether a test item was a plant.
- I wrote an **operational definition** of a plant.

You will learn:

- how the shape and size of a cell are related to its function.
- how other differences in structure are related to a cell's function.

Lesson 4

How Do Cells Differ?

How do you think the cells in the body of a dog compare with the cells in the body of the flea that sits on it? Are the dog's body cells bigger than those of the flea? Or are there just more cells in the dog's body?

Cell Shape and Size

You've learned that all cells have similar parts and that plant cells have some parts that animal cells do not. There are many other differences among the cells of different kinds of organisms. In fact, there are even differences among the cells of the same many-celled organism.

These Wandering Jew leaves are made of several different kinds of tissues. Each tissue is made of groups of similar cells that perform a similar function. The photo shows cells that cover the leaf of the plant. ▼

magnification x60

Look at the pictures to the left. The cells you see in the top picture cover the outer part of the leaf on the plant. These cells protect the leaf. The shapes of these cells help them fit together tightly so that they cover the other cells inside the leaf completely.

Now look at the photo of the leaf cells again. Do you see the bean-shaped cells that occur in pairs? These cells are called guard cells. They allow gases such as oxygen and carbon dioxide to enter and exit the leaf. How does the shape of these cells help them do this job?

As you can see, the shape of a cell helps it perform a specific function within an organism. On the next page, you can see the shapes of some of the 100 different cells within the human body.

Human Body Cells

Skin

Skin cells cover and protect your body. They keep harmful organisms from entering your body. The lifespan of a skin cell is 19-34 days.

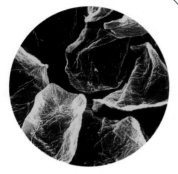

magnification x4,800

Blood

Notice the difference in shape between these red blood cells and white blood cells. Red blood cells live about 120 days. They carry oxygen to your body cells and carry wastes away. White blood cells, which live from several hours to several years, protect you from disease.

magnification x4,800

Nerve

Long, narrow nerve cells carry messages—from one cell to the next—throughout your body. Nerve cells live for the lifetime of the individual. How does the shape of this nerve cell enable it to carry on its functions?

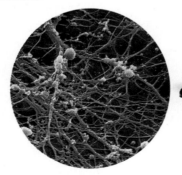

magnification x5,920

Muscle

Muscle cells work together to help you move, to push food through your digestive system, and to keep your heart beating. The long, thin shape of these cells allows them to contract to move parts of your body. Their lifespan can be as long as the lifespan of the organism.

magnification x560

Here's one example of how the shape of cells in your body helps them do their job. When bacteria invade your body, the white blood cells take action. Their job is to find and destroy the invaders. White blood cells are irregularly shaped. Their shape allows them to slip through the thin walls of blood vessels and move among your muscle cells and other tissues. Do you see how this would help them find the invaders in your body?

You might think that one-celled organisms are similar to each other, but they too have a large variety of shapes. A single cell must carry out the same jobs that are carried out by all the cells of many-celled organisms like you. Notice how the one-celled organisms pictured below have different cell shapes that allow them to survive in their environment.

Vorticella lives in ponds attached to solid objects, such as twigs. Notice the special funnel shape of this one-celled organism. The small hair-like structures, called cilia, around the top of the funnel in vorticella beat, creating a whirlpool. Microscopic food particles are swept into the funnel and drawn into the vorticella.

The shape of the vorticella helps it feed and, therefore, survive in its environment. ▼

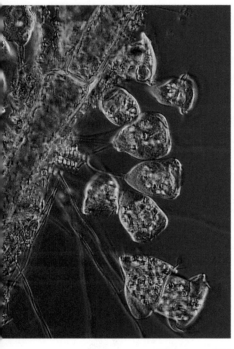

magnification x151

Thousands of volvox cells group together to form a hollow sphere filled with water. Inside these spheres, new colonies are forming. ▼

magnification x550

◄ *The ameba constantly changes shape as it extends pseudopods to flow from place to place.*

magnification x1710

Amebas live on the bottom of bodies of water. An ameba has no definite shape. It moves by pushing out its cytoplasm into thin pouches in the cell membrane. These pouches are called pseudopods, which means "false feet." An ameba feeds on small organisms by flowing around them. Once a pseudopod surrounds the food, the ameba digests it.

Volvox live in fresh water and form hollow balls. Each ball contains from 500 to 50,000 cells. Although the cells of Volvox group together, they do not form a tissue. Each of the green cells makes its own sugars. Each of the cells has a pair of whiplike structures called flagella. When all the cells in the group move their flagella together, the ball of cells moves by rolling over and over.

Cells vary in size as well as shape. Does that mean that large organisms have large cells? Not always. Think of yourself as a baby. You were made of many cells of different tissues. However, you didn't grow bigger because your cells got bigger. Instead, your bone cells produced more bone cells to make longer, bigger bones. Your skin cells produced more skin cells to make your skin cover more area. The number of cells in your body increased, not the size. In fact, an adult human body has about 100 trillion cells.

Cells within your body differ in size, and cells in different organisms differ in size. As the picture shows, bacteria are among the smallest cells. A nerve cell in the giraffe is one of the longest cells. The cell with the largest volume of all is so large that you don't even need a microscope to see it—the yolk of an ostrich egg.

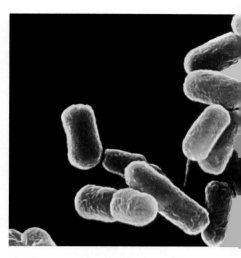

▲ Bacteria, like the Escherichia coli *pictured above, are some of the smallest cells in the world. These cells are magnified 3,700 times.*

Cells vary greatly in size. The nerve cell that runs from the giraffe's hip to its toe is almost 6 meters long! ▶

6 m

A29

Other Differences in Structure

The function that a cell performs determines the kinds and number of organelles it has. For example, a muscle cell in your leg has to contract quickly as you stand, walk, and run. It contains a greater number of energy-producing mitochondria than a bone cell does. Think about the constantly active cells in your heart and the cells that make up the growing layers of your skin. Which would have more mitochondria?

Some cells have special outgrowths from their membranes. Flagella extend from volvox and help them move. The vorticella has hairlike structures called cilia on top of its funnel. The cilia move rapidly to create the whirlpool that helps the vorticella feed. The pictures on this page also show other cells with cilia. The cells that line your breathing passages, lungs, and nose have hundreds of cilia. Their motion helps keep your air passages clean. On a single-celled paramecium, the cilia beat rhythmically, moving the paramecium through the water in which it lives.

▲ Cilia that line your windpipe carry mucus and trapped dust upward toward your throat. These cilia have been magnified 4,170 times.

magnification x4500

▲ Cilia on a slipper-shaped paramecium allow it to move from place to place and help it feed.

Lesson 4 Review

1. How is the shape and size of a cell related to its function?

2. What other differences in a cell are related to its function?

3. **Bar Graphs**
   How do the lifespans of different cells vary? Use the information on page A27 to make a bar graph that answers this question.

Experimenting with Membranes

Materials

- safety goggles
- 6 plastic graduated cups
- water
- sugar test strips with key
- clock
- dropper
- iodine solution
- sugar solution
- starch solution
- masking tape
- marker
- scissors
- dialysis tubing
- metric ruler
- 6 pieces of string
- funnel
- paper towel

Process Skills

- formulating questions and hypotheses
- identifying and controlling variables
- making and using models
- experimenting
- estimating and measuring
- observing
- collecting and interpreting data
- communicating

Process Skills

State the Problem

What dissolved materials pass through a membrane?

Formulate Your Hypothesis

If cell models containing starch and sugar solutions are placed in plain water, which substances will pass through the membrane into the water? Write your **hypothesis.**

Identify and Control the Variables

To see which materials will pass through a membrane, you must control the variables. The dissolved substance is the **variable** that changes in this experiment. You will use three cell **models.** One cell will contain only water. A second cell will contain starch solution, and the third will contain sugar solution. Remember to keep all other variables the same.

Test Your Hypothesis

Follow these steps to perform an **experiment.**

1 Put on your safety goggles. Make a chart like the one on page A33. Use your chart to record your observations.

Photo A

Continued →

2 **Measure** 30 mL of water in a plastic graduated cup. Place a sugar test strip in the water for about 15 seconds. Remove the strip and wait 1 minute. Compare the color of the tip of the test strip with the key (Photo A). Record your **observations.** Add 3 drops of iodine solution to the same cup of water. Record your observations.

⚠️ *Safety Note Handle iodine solution carefully. Do not get iodine on skin or clothing.*

3 Repeat step 2 with the sugar solution. Repeat step 2 with the starch solution.

4 Use tape and a marker to label 3 plastic cups *Control, Starch,* and *Sugar.* Fill the cups with water until each is about two-thirds full. Each cup should contain the same amount of water.

5 Use scissors to cut 3 pieces of dialysis tubing, each about 12 cm in length. Soak the tubing in a cup of water for 1 minute. Remove the tubing from the water and tie one end of each piece with a string. Be sure to tie the string tightly.

6 Use a funnel to add water to the open end of one tied tube. Then tightly tie the tube with string (Photo B). Place the tube in the cup of water marked *Control.*

7 Fill a second tube with starch solution. Tie the other end of the tube with a string and rinse the outside carefully. Place it in the cup of water labeled *Starch.*

8 Clean the funnel with a paper towel. Repeat step 7 using sugar solution. Place the tube in the cup of water labeled *Sugar* (Photo C).

9 Allow the tubes to remain in the cups of water overnight. Remove the tubes from the cups. Use a sugar test strip to test the liquid in all 3 cups. **Collect data** by recording your observations. Use a dropper to place 3 drops of iodine solution in each cup. Record your observations.

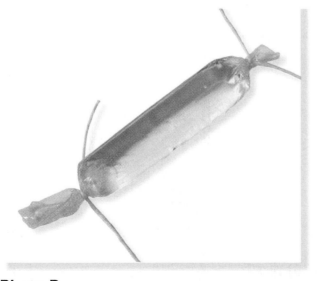

Photo B

Photo C

Collect Your Data

	Sugar test strip	Iodine solution
Water (step 2)		
Starch solution (step 3)		
Sugar solution (step 3)		
Liquid in *Control* cup		
Liquid in *Starch* cup		
Liquid in *Sugar* cup		

Interpret Your Data

Use your data. How can you tell if a solution contains starch? How can you tell if it contains sugar? Which cups in step 9 contained solutions with sugar? Which contained solutions with starch?

State Your Conclusion

Study your data. How do your results compare with your hypothesis? **Communicate** your results. Tell which materials, if any, can pass through a membrane.

Inquire Further

Does the amount of sugar or starch dissolved in the water in the cell affect the experiment results? Develop a plan to answer this or other questions you may have.

Self-Assessment

- I formulated a **hypothesis**.
- I **experimented** to see which materials will pass through a membrane.
- I **controlled variables**.
- I **collected** and **interpreted data**.
- I **communicated** my results.

Chapter 1 Review

Chapter Main Ideas

Lesson 1
• A species is a group of organisms that have the same characteristics and can produce similar offspring that can also reproduce.
• The invention of the compound and electron microscopes enabled scientists to learn about cells.
• The cell theory states that the cell is the basic unit of all living organisms, and only living cells can produce new living cells.

Lesson 2
• The main parts of an animal cell are the nucleus, cell membrane, and cytoplasm.
• Structures called organelles inside the cytoplasm carry on different functions for the cell.

Lesson 3
• Parts of a plant cell include the cell membrane, nucleus, cytoplasm, and organelles, including chloroplasts, and a tough outer support called a cell wall.
• Through photosynthesis plants give off oxygen and make sugars that store energy. Other organisms need these materials to survive.

Lesson 4
• The shape and size of a cell is related to its specific function within an organism.
• The function of a cell is related to the kinds and number of organelles it has.

Reviewing Science Words and Concepts

Write the letter of the word or phrase that best completes each sentence.

a. cell membrane
b. cell theory
c. cell wall
d. chlorophyll
e. chloroplast
f. chromosome
g. compound microscope
h. cytoplasm
i. endoplasmic reticulum
j. mitochondria
k. nucleus
l. organelle
m. ribosome
n. species
o. vacuole

1. All dogs are members of the same ___.
2. An instrument using two lenses for magnifying objects is a(n) ___.
3. According to the ___, all organisms are made of one or more cells.
4. The control center of a living cell is the ___.
5. A structure in the nucleus that carries information that controls cell activities is the ___.
6. A thin, flexible protective cell covering is the ___.
7. The jellylike material filling the space between the cell membrane and the nucleus is ___.
8. Ribosomes, mitochondria, and vacuoles are examples of a(n) ___.

9. Organelles in the cytoplasm where energy is released are ___.

10. A saclike organelle where a cell's food and water are stored is a(n) ___.

11. An organelle for transporting materials inside the cell is the ___.

12. Part of a cell that puts together proteins for the cell is the ___.

13. Green substance in plant cells is ___.

14. An organelle that makes sugar is the ___.

15. The tough outer support of a plant cell is the ___.

Explaining Science

Create a comparison chart or write a paragraph that explains these questions.

1. How do various species differ?

2. How do the parts of an animal cell function?

3. How do plant and animal cells differ?

4. What are the differences in the cells within an organism?

Using Skills

1. The actual number of species on Earth is unknown because scientists continue to identify new species. The table shows the total number of bird species that were known in three different years. Convert this information to a **bar graph**.

Year	Number of known species
1758	360
1845	4500
1990	9000

2. Make a list of at least 10 different species you are familiar with. **Classify** the species into groups according to their characteristics. Identify the characteristics of each group.

3. On page A13, you read about the experiment of a Belgian doctor in the 1600s to show that mice develop from wheat. Describe an experiment to prove the doctor's theory wrong. **Identify** the **variables**.

Critical Thinking

1. Compare and **contrast** the similarities and differences in the characteristics among species of pets owned by classmates.

2. Imagine looking at an unknown cell through an electron microscope. How might you apply what you know about cell structure to **infer** whether the cell is from a plant or animal?

3. Compare and **contrast** the human body cells pictured on page A27. **Draw a conclusion** about how the shape of each cell makes it well suited to its function.

The Pick of the Litter

Which puppy would you like? Each one is unique. Where in the world did the variety of physical characteristics in these puppies come from?

Chapter 2
Reproduction and Heredity

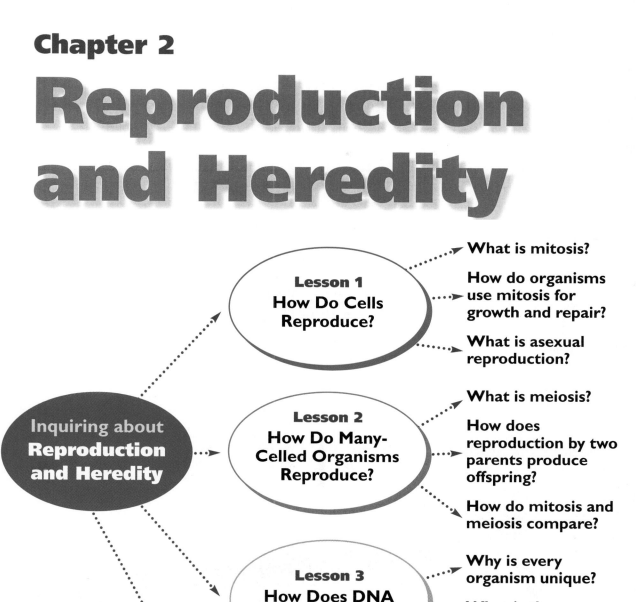

Inquiring about Reproduction and Heredity

Lesson 1
How Do Cells Reproduce?

- What is mitosis?
- How do organisms use mitosis for growth and repair?
- What is asexual reproduction?

Lesson 2
How Do Many-Celled Organisms Reproduce?

- What is meiosis?
- How does reproduction by two parents produce offspring?
- How do mitosis and meiosis compare?

Lesson 3
How Does DNA Control Traits?

- Why is every organism unique?
- What is the structure of DNA?
- How does DNA make copies of itself?
- How is DNA information used?

Lesson 4
How Do Organisms Inherit Traits?

- How does sexual reproduction produce variations in offspring?
- What are dominant and recessive genes?
- How can mutations affect an organism?

Copy the chapter graphic organizer onto your own paper. This organizer shows you what the whole chapter is all about. As you read the lessons and do the activities, look for answers to the questions and write them on your organizer.

Exploring Variation in Species

Process Skills

Process Skills

- observing
- estimating and measuring
- communicating
- inferring

Materials

- 10 peanuts in the shell
- metric ruler
- graph paper

Explore

1 Make a chart like the one shown. Use your chart to record your observations.

Peanut	Observations	Length
1		
2		
3		

2 **Observe** 10 peanut shells closely. Record your observations. What differences do you notice?

3 **Measure** the length of the 10 peanut shells to the nearest millimeter. Record your measurements.

4 Combine your data with the data of the other groups.

5 Make a bar graph that shows the data collected by your group and a bar graph that shows the combined class data. Label the graphs as shown.

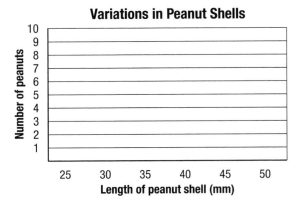

Variations in Peanut Shells

Number of peanuts

Length of peanut shell (mm)

Reflect

1. What can you **infer** about the variation within a species on the basis of your observations?

2. Compare your group's graph with the class data. Which graph shows a greater variation? Why do you think this is so? **Communicate** your ideas to the class.

? **Inquire Further**

Do other species show similar variation? Develop a plan to answer this or other questions you may have.

Metric Conversions

Height is one trait that you inherit from your parents. You can use the metric system to measure height.

The base unit for measuring height (length) in the metric system is the **meter**. You can convert the meter to different units to describe amounts that are longer or shorter.

Math Vocabulary

meter, the basic unit of length in the metric system

Example

Name	Abbreviation	Number of Base Units	Approximate Comparison
Kilometer	km	1,000	9 football fields
Meter	m	1	Half the height of a door
Centimeter	cm	$\frac{1}{100}$	Length of a raisin
Millimeter	mm	$\frac{1}{1000}$	Width of a period at the end of a sentence

Look at the chart. Notice that to convert a unit, you multiply or divide by a power of 10. For example, to convert from a kilometer to a meter, you multiply by 1,000 $\frac{m}{km}$.

1 km x 1,000 $\frac{m}{km}$ = 1,000 m

To convert from centimeters to meters, you divide by 100 $\frac{cm}{m}$.

200 cm ÷ 100 $\frac{cm}{m}$ = 2 m

Talk About It!

1. Can any measurement in millimeters be converted to meters? Explain.

2. Why is it more appropriate to measure your height in centimeters than in meters?

Did you know?

The meter was originally defined as $\frac{1}{10,000,000}$ of the distance from the equator to the North Pole. It took the French from 1792 to 1798 to measure this distance. Today's satellites confirm that their measurements were only off by 0.2 mm.

What's the Big Idea?

You will learn:

- what mitosis is.
- how organisms use mitosis for growth and repair.
- what asexual reproduction is.

Glossary

Glossary

mitosis (mī tō′ sis), the process by which a cell produces two new identical nuclei

cell division (sel də vizh′ ən), the dividing of a cell following mitosis

Your body produces 32 million new red blood cells like this every day! ▼

Lesson 1

How Do Cells Reproduce?

Wow! That sunflower plant sure grew a lot since last week. It must be a meter tall already. How did it get so big so fast? Are its cells just getting fatter? Maybe it just has more cells. But where did they come from?

Mitosis

All over the world, the cells of organisms—single-celled organisms, plants, animals, even your own body—are dividing to produce new cells. How does this happen?

You learned in Chapter 1 that the nucleus of a cell contains chromosomes. Each species has a certain number of chromosomes in its body cells. Humans have 46 chromosomes in each body cell, bullfrogs have 26, chickens have 78, and an onion plant has 32.

Before one cell divides into two cells, it makes copies of all its chromosomes. What would happen if a cell didn't copy its chromosomes before dividing?

After the chromosomes are copied, the cell goes through a process called mitosis. During **mitosis,** the cell's nucleus divides to form two identical nuclei. Mitosis is a continuous process. However, to make it easier to understand, scientists often describe it as a series of steps. You can see these steps on the next page.

After mitosis, a cell divides in two in a process called **cell division.** Two new offspring cells are formed. After cell division, each of the two new cells has one of the nuclei that formed during mitosis. Therefore, each new cell has a complete set of chromosomes. The chromosomes are the same in both offspring cells, and they are the same as in the parent cell. All your body cells were formed—and some, like the red blood cell in the picture, are forming right now—by mitosis and cell division.

Mitosis

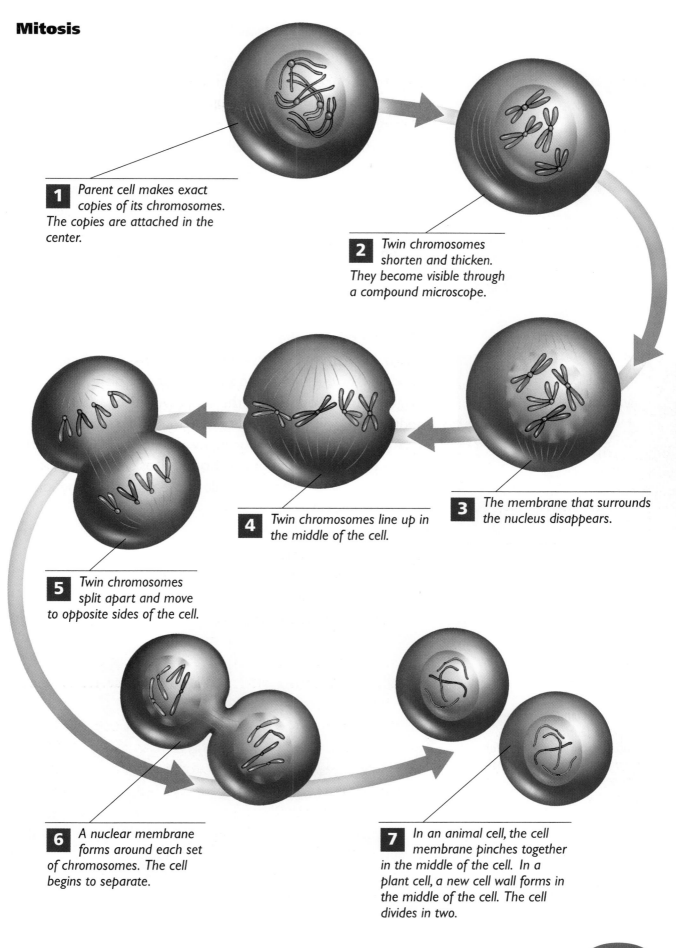

1 Parent cell makes exact copies of its chromosomes. The copies are attached in the center.

2 Twin chromosomes shorten and thicken. They become visible through a compound microscope.

3 The membrane that surrounds the nucleus disappears.

4 Twin chromosomes line up in the middle of the cell.

5 Twin chromosomes split apart and move to opposite sides of the cell.

6 A nuclear membrane forms around each set of chromosomes. The cell begins to separate.

7 In an animal cell, the cell membrane pinches together in the middle of the cell. In a plant cell, a new cell wall forms in the middle of the cell. The cell divides in two.

Growth and Repair

Your growth is just one example of what happens when cells reproduce. You are much taller now than when you were born. You grew largely because of mitosis and cell division. When you are fully grown, your body will contain about 100 trillion cells! Cell reproduction, therefore, results in the growth of organisms.

Have you ever planted a sunflower seed and watched it grow into a tall plant like the one in the picture? Each seed contains a partially developed plant called an embryo. When the embryo swells, grows, and breaks out of the seed, a young plant called a seedling forms. The seedling grows as new cells are constantly made.

The first part of the seedling to start growing is the root. Then the shoot—the part of the plant that makes the stems, leaves, and flowers—begins to grow. New cells produced at the tips of the stems make the plant grow bigger. Throughout its life, the sunflower plant grows by adding new cells at the end of its roots and shoots.

Animals grow by producing new cells too. Consider the kitten below. Throughout its body, mitosis produces new cells. Many of these cells result in the growth of the kitten into an adult cat.

▲ Mitosis in this plant produces new cells for growth.

This kitten could live more than 20 years. During that time, mitosis produces new cells for growth and repair of the cat's body cells. ▶

Mitosis and cell division also result in the replacement of old cells that have died and in the repair of cell tissue. For example, the outer layer of your skin is made up of dead cells that continually flake off. Below these dead cells are cube-shaped cells that form new skin cells. These new cells continually move up to the surface and replace the worn-out cells. The skin covering your entire body is replaced about once every month.

The cells that line your stomach are constantly bathed in strong acid that helps you digest food. Because they live in such a harsh environment, your stomach-lining cells are replaced about every two days.

Your blood contains different kinds of cells. Red blood cells, which carry oxygen, live only about 120 days. Then they die. White blood cells help defend your body against disease. They can live from a few hours to several years. Your body is constantly making both red and white blood cells to replace those that die.

Platelets are a third kind of cell found in your blood. They live for about ten days. In the cut finger shown in the picture, platelets come in contact with the ends of the broken blood vessels. They swell and stick to the rough surface of the cut and to one another. In this way, platelets help a clot form to stop the bleeding. In time, the injury is repaired by the growth of new cells. These cells replace those that were damaged by the cut.

Plants also produce new cells for repair. For example, you have probably seen branches broken off from trees after a violent storm. When this damage happens, the tree makes new cells that gradually cover and repair the wound. What happens to grass after it is mowed?

If you cut your finger, new cells will eventually grow to heal the cut. ▼

▲ *These platelets help stop bleeding in two ways. They form a plug by sticking to the tears in a blood vessel. They also release a substance that causes fibrin, the stringy material in the picture, to be produced. What do you think the function of fibrin is?*

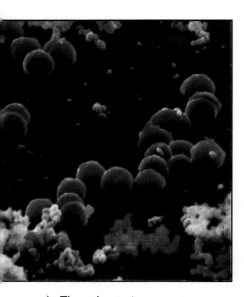

Glossary

asexual reproduction
(ā sek´ shü əl rē prə duk´ shən), reproduction by one parent

These bacteria can enter your body through injury to your skin. Once they're in your body, the bacteria can cause several diseases.

Bud —

— Parent cell

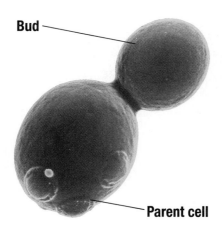

The tiny holes you see in bread result from the bubbles made by microscopic organisms like the one you see here. These organisms, called yeasts, belong to a group of organisms known as fungi. This process in which yeasts reproduce asexually is called budding.

Asexual Reproduction

You just learned that, in many-celled organisms such as you, cell reproduction leads to new body cells. But did you know that in one-celled organisms, cell reproduction leads to new organisms? The process in which a new organism is produced by just one parent is called **asexual reproduction** .

The pictures below show a one-celled ameba reproducing. After mitosis and cell division, you can see the two new amebas that are produced. Both these amebas are identical to the parent ameba because their chromosomes are identical.

Many other single-celled organisms also reproduce asexually. Bacteria are single-celled organisms that cause many illnesses, such as strep throat and pneumonia. Bacteria are also used to make vinegar, yogurt, cheese, pickles, and other food products. Bacterial cells, like those in the picture to the left, do not have a nucleus. However, they do have a single, loop-shaped chromosome. When a bacterium reproduces, it makes a copy of its chromosome. Then the cell divides in two. As with the ameba, the two bacteria are identical to the parent.

The organism in the photo to the lower left is a yeast. Bakers add yeast to the dough that bread is made from. The yeast causes the bread to rise. Yeast cells reproduce asexually. After a yeast cell's nucleus has completed mitosis, a small part of the parent cell begins to pinch off. The cytoplasm, the clear, jellylike substance that fills the cell, divides unequally. The smaller part, called

2 When a single-celled ameba reaches a certain size, it gets ready to divide.

1 An ameba reproduces by asexual reproduction.

a bud, at first stays attached to the parent cell. Then it grows and eventually separates from the parent to live on its own. The parent cell and the new cell are identical because their chromosomes are identical.

At times, some many-celled organisms also reproduce asexually. For example, a ribbon worm sometimes attaches its tail to a rock or other hard surface. It then crawls in the opposite direction. Eventually, its body tears in half. Each half will grow into a complete worm by making new cells. The new individuals are identical to the original organism.

In the spring, potato farmers get ready for planting. They cut potatoes into pieces so that each piece has an "eye." After planting, each eye develops into a new plant. From one potato, a number of new plants are formed. Each plant has chromosomes that are exactly like those of the original potato.

3 *After the nucleus of the ameba has undergone mitosis, cell division begins.*

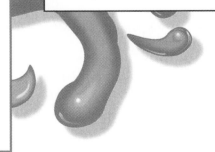

4 *Following cell division, two new amebas are formed. These new cells are identical to the parent cell.*

Lesson 1 Review

1. What is mitosis?

2. Give examples of how organisms use mitosis for growth and repair.

3. What is asexual reproduction?

4. **Metric Conversions**
   A human body has about 4 liters of blood. How many milliliters of blood does a human body have?

A 45

What's the Big Idea?

You will learn:

- what meiosis is.
- how reproduction by two parents produces offspring.
- how mitosis and meiosis compare.

Glossary

Glossary

sexual reproduction (sek′shü əl rē prə duk′ shən), reproduction by two parents

sex cell (seks sel), a type of cell produced only by an organism that reproduces sexually

meiosis (mī ō′ sis), the process by which sex cells form

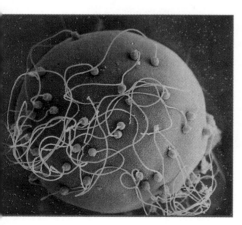

▲ Many sperm cells surround this egg cell. However, only one sperm cell will unite with the egg cell.

Lesson 2

How Do Many-Celled Organisms Reproduce?

They're so cute! At your friend's house is a new litter of puppies. The mother dog is a black poodle, and the father dog is a white, short-haired terrier. What do you think the puppies will look like? Will they look more like the mother or the father?

Meiosis

When a litter of puppies is born, none of the puppies will be identical to its mother or father. That is because the puppies are the result of **sexual reproduction**, or the reproduction by two parents. Dogs, and other organisms that reproduce sexually, have special cells called **sex cells**. Each puppy results when one sex cell from the mother joins with one sex cell from the father. The sex cell that comes from the female parent is an egg cell. The sex cell that comes from the male parent is a sperm cell. You can see sperm cells surrounding an egg cell in the photo. Notice that the sperm cells are much smaller than the egg cell.

Unlike body cells, sex cells form by a process called **meiosis**. Sex cells have only half the number of chromosomes as the parent cell. Follow the process on the next page as you read how this happens.

Before meiosis begins, each chromosome duplicates itself, forming twin chromosomes. Meiosis itself occurs in two stages. During the first stage of meiosis (steps 1–5), the twin chromosomes separate, and the cell divides. Two cells are the result. Each has the same number of chromosomes as the first cell.

During the second stage of meiosis (steps 6–10), the chromosomes in each cell split apart, and each cell divides. Four cells are formed. Each has half the number of chromosomes as the first cell.

Meiosis

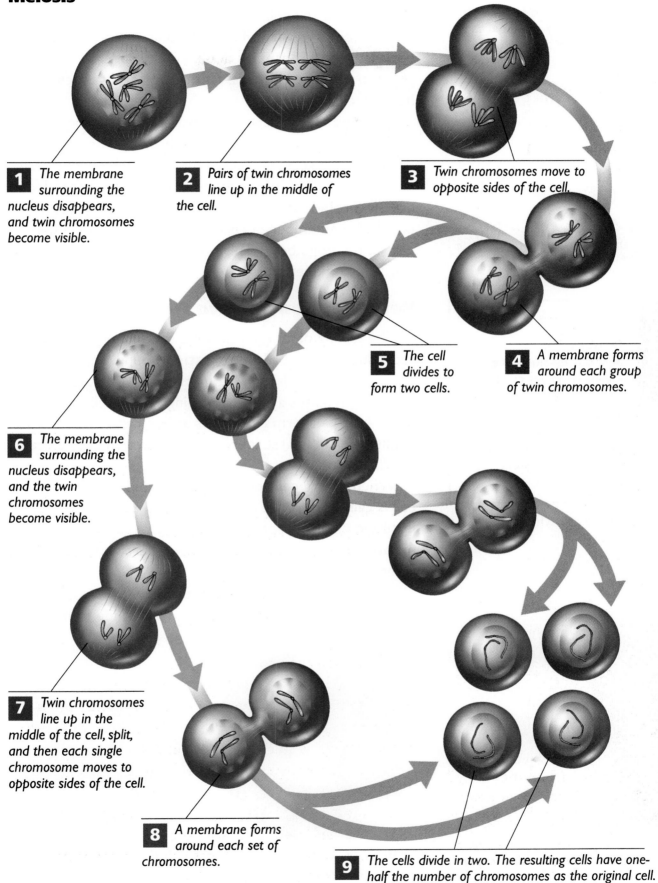

1 The membrane surrounding the nucleus disappears, and twin chromosomes become visible.

2 Pairs of twin chromosomes line up in the middle of the cell.

3 Twin chromosomes move to opposite sides of the cell.

4 A membrane forms around each group of twin chromosomes.

5 The cell divides to form two cells.

6 The membrane surrounding the nucleus disappears, and the twin chromosomes become visible.

7 Twin chromosomes line up in the middle of the cell, split, and then each single chromosome moves to opposite sides of the cell.

8 A membrane forms around each set of chromosomes.

9 The cells divide in two. The resulting cells have one-half the number of chromosomes as the original cell.

Meiosis in Dogs

This diagram shows how the number of chromosomes in each cell changes as sex cells are produced. ▼

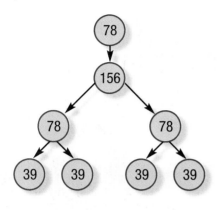

Glossary

Glossary

fertilization
(fėr´ tl ə zā´ shən), the joining of an egg cell and a sperm cell during sexual reproduction

zygote (zī´ gōt), the first cell of an offspring, formed when an egg cell and a sperm cell join

Think back to the litter of puppies. Each resulted from the joining of sex cells from two parents. A dog has 78 chromosomes in each of its body cells. Before meiosis begins, the chromosomes double in the special cell that is going to produce sex cells. At that point, this parent cell has 156 chromosomes.

During the first stage of meiosis, the cell divides in two. Each of the two new cells has 78 chromosomes.

During the second stage of meiosis, each of those cells divides again. Each of the four sex cells that are produced has 39 chromosomes. In other words, each sex cell has only half the number of chromosomes as do the other cells in the dog's body. This process is summarized in the diagram to the left.

Reproduction by Two Parents

The joining of an egg cell and a sperm cell during sexual reproduction is called **fertilization**. Suppose, for example, a female frog lays a mass of eggs in water. The male frog releases a fluid containing sperm cells over the eggs. When a sperm cell enters an egg cell, fertilization results. Only the first sperm cell to enter an egg cell can fertilize that egg.

When an egg cell and a sperm cell join, the resulting cell is called a **zygote**. The first picture below shows the fertilized egg, or zygote, of a frog. The zygote undergoes mitosis and cell division to form two cells within two to three hours after fertilization.

The two cells that were produced by the zygote then divide to form four cells. The four cells divide to become

Frog Development

These microscopic photos show how a single-celled frog zygote divides to produce more cells. The cells will continue to divide many times until a multicellular tadpole is hatched. ▶

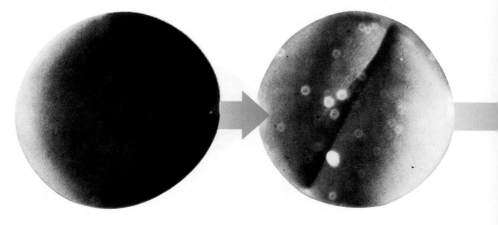

Zygote

eight cells, and so on. You can see this ongoing development of the frog in the next three pictures. Mitosis and cell division continue, with each new cell producing more cells. After a period of six to nine days, a complete tadpole has formed.

The young alligator in the picture resulted from sexual reproduction. Unlike the egg cells of frogs, alligator egg cells are fertilized by the male parent's sperm inside the female parent's body. After fertilization occurs, a leathery covering forms over each zygote. These fertilized zygotes develop into eggs, which the female lays in a large nest on the bank of a pond or river. In about 60 days, the zygote in each egg has developed into a many-celled organism, and the young alligator hatches. The newly hatched alligator is much smaller than its parents. How will the alligator grow to adult size?

In most mammals, not only does fertilization take place within the female's body, but development of the offspring does too. Like the mother dog at your friend's house, most female mammals give birth to live young.

▲ *As in all cases of sexual reproduction, this young alligator started out as a single cell.*

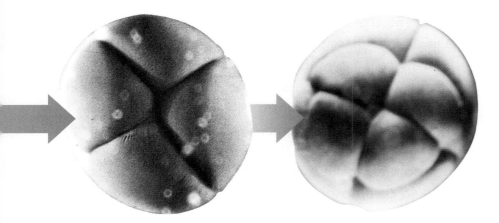

Stamen with pollen

Pistil

▲ *Flowers are organs of sexual reproduction. In many plants, both male and female sex cells are produced in the same flower.*

▲ *How do these kittens look like their parent? How do they differ from their parent and from one another?*

Animals aren't the only organisms to reproduce by sexual reproduction. Plants do too. Flowers, such as this lily to the left, are the reproductive organs of a plant. In flowering plants, the male sex cells are in the pollen. Pollen is produced by the flower's stamen. The female egg cells are formed at the base of the female part of the flower called the pistil. The male sex cells travel down the pistil, where they fertilize the eggs, forming zygotes. A protective covering forms around the zygote, resulting in a seed. The seed protects the developing organism.

There's an important difference between sexual and asexual reproduction. The kittens in this picture resulted from sexual reproduction. What do you notice about their appearance? Compare each kitten with its parent. You'll see that its coloring is different from that of the mother. That difference is a result of sexual reproduction. The mother's egg cell contributed half the chromosomes that the kitten has. The father's sperm cell contributed the other half. Therefore, the kittens are not exactly like either their mother or their father. How does this result differ from the offspring produced during asexual reproduction?

Comparing Mitosis and Meiosis

Important differences exist between mitosis and meiosis. The chart on the next page makes it easier to picture and compare these two processes and their results.

In many-celled organisms, mitosis occurs in body cells and leads to new body cells. Meiosis occurs in special cells to produce sex cells. The main difference between body cells and sex cells is the number of chromosomes in their nuclei. All body cells have the normal number of chromosomes for the species. For example, a human body cell has 46 chromosomes. Sex cells have half the number of normal chromosomes for the species. A human egg cell and a human sperm cell each have 23 chromosomes.

Parent cell with 2 chromosomes	Chromosomes doubled	Chromosomes separate	Cell divides in two	Cells divide in two again

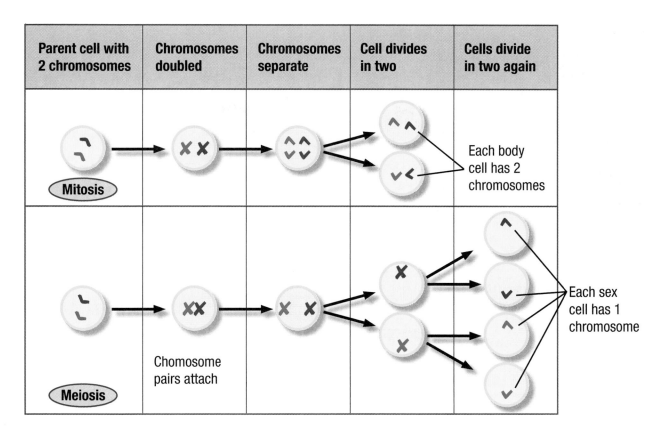

The number of chromosomes in body cells and sex cells differs because the number of divisions in mitosis and meiosis differs. In mitosis, the cell divides once. During meiosis, two divisions occur.

Finally, because the number of chromosomes differs, the offspring that result differ too. Mitosis leads to offspring that are identical to the parent because their chromosomes are identical. Meiosis leads to offspring that are not identical because their chromosomes are not identical to either parent's chromosomes.

Lesson 2 Review

1. What is meiosis?
2. How does reproduction by two parents produce offspring?
3. How do mitosis and meiosis compare?
4. **Metric Conversions**
   A human fetus grows by the process of mitosis from 0.02 cm at 6 days to about 46 cm at birth. Convert these measurements to millimeters.

What's the **Big Idea?**

You will learn:

- why every organism is unique.
- what the structure of DNA is.
- how DNA makes copies of itself.
- how DNA information is used.

Glossary

trait (trāt), a characteristic of an organism

DNA, the molecule in each cell that directs the cell's activities

Look at these animals around a waterhole in Namibia, Africa. What characteristics do the animals share? Are they members of the same species? How do you know? ▼

How Does DNA Control Traits?

Look in a mirror. **WOW!** Who is that you see? Did you know that the person you see is unique? That means "one of a kind," and that's what you are. Why? The answer lies within your cells.

Unique DNA

If you were asked to contrast the animals in the picture, what would you say? You might recognize that some of the animals are giraffes and some are zebras. Recall what you learned in Chapter 1 about species. The giraffes belong to a species that is different from the species that the zebras belong to. Each animal has all the physical characteristics, or **traits**, of the species to which it belongs.

How do the traits of these giraffes and zebras differ? The giraffes have longer necks and legs than those of the zebras. The colors and patterns on the body of each group are also different. Their differences, however, are more than in just the way they look.

Inside the nucleus of each giraffe cell is a set of instructions for building the giraffe's body. Those instructions are found in the giraffe's chromosomes. You've already learned that chromosomes are the parts of a cell's nucleus that carry information that controls all the cell's activities. Chromosomes contain a substance called **DNA**—<u>d</u>eoxyribo<u>n</u>ucleic <u>a</u>cid. The DNA determines the kind of organism that the cell belongs to—in this case, a giraffe.

Glossary

The DNA of a chromosome is divided into sections called genes. Each **gene** controls how a certain trait will develop. For example, a gene might control the color of a giraffe's hair. A giraffe's body develops and works in certain ways because of the particular genes that the zygote received from the parents during fertilization.

Giraffes and zebras are more alike than giraffes and dogs. This means that giraffes and zebras share more of the same genes than do giraffes and dogs. Yet their genes are different enough that they belong to separate species.

How do the genes of the giraffes in the picture compare? Since the giraffes are all members of the same species, they share most of the same genes. However, the giraffes are not exactly alike. Each giraffe has a slightly different combination of genes that makes it a one-of-a-kind giraffe.

No two living things that are produced by sexual reproduction—except identical twins—have exactly the same genes. The cells in an organism's body carry a chemical pattern of DNA that makes it different from every other organism. What are some traits that make you unique?

Glossary

gene (jēn), a section of DNA on a chromosome that controls a trait

Glossary

DNA

Long, twisted strands of DNA make up the chromosomes in a cell's nucleus. In fact, the DNA is coiled so tightly that if the DNA in a single chromosome could be stretched out, it would be up to 10,000 times longer than the chromosome itself. Follow this DNA strand on the following pages. ▼

— Cell nucleus

— Chromosome

— DNA

Structure of DNA

More than a hundred years ago, **History of Science** biologists first observed chromosomes. Later, they suggested that genes were located on chromosomes. It wasn't until 1953 that two scientists, James Watson of the United States and Francis Crick of Great Britain, discovered the structure of chromosomal DNA. Their discovery helped scientists understand how the structure of DNA allows it to make copies of itself. From this discovery, scientists were able to better understand how traits can be passed from parent to offspring. In 1962, Watson and Crick received a Nobel Prize for their model of DNA.

You can take a closer look at models of DNA molecules on this page and the following pages. Each chromosome inside the nucleus of a cell is a long, tightly coiled strand of DNA.

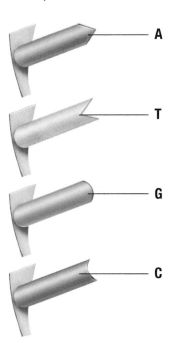

Glossary

base (bās), one kind of molecule that makes up a DNA strand

DNA Bases

DNA is made of four different kinds of bases. ▼

A

T

G

C

The shape of the DNA molecule looks like a long, twisted ladder. The ladder has millions of rungs made of four kinds of smaller molecules called **bases**. The four bases are represented by the letters *A, T, G,* and *C.* Bases have shapes that allow them to fit together only in certain combinations. Find the rungs in the diagram. Notice the color combinations that appear. Use the key to the left to see which bases fit together.

The bases pair up in this way to form the rungs of the ladder. The order in which the base pairs are arranged determines what instructions the cell receives. Notice that the arrangement of the base pairs varies from place to place on the chromosome. Different segments of the DNA ladder—genes—have different sequences of base pairs.

The differences in the sequences of base pairs in the genes allow the genes to give the cell an almost endless set of instructions for controlling all the characteristics of the individual. For example, an arrangement of GC-TA-CG-GC, which is shown on the DNA segment below, will give a different set of instructions to the cell than the arrangement shown on the next page, which is GC-TA-AT-GC.

DNA Structure

A DNA molecule looks like a twisted ladder. The ladder has millions of rungs. ▼

G

C

T

A

C

G

G

C

Gene

The DNA ladder has sections called genes. A DNA ladder has thousands of genes, which can be from a few hundred to a few thousand rungs long.

The DNA on all the chromosomes of an organism carries all the information about that organism's traits. For example, certain genes in your cells carry the information that determines the shape of your body. Likewise, instructions for the formation of a giraffe's body are contained in the DNA in the giraffe's cells. Every cell in the giraffe's body carries that same information.

Why is the information coded in the DNA of a giraffe so different from the information in your cells? After all, the same four bases—A, T, G, and C—make up the DNA of all living organisms. The information is different because the way in which the base pairs are arranged on the rungs of the DNA ladder is different in a giraffe than it is in your body cells. It is the unique arrangement of base pairs in DNA that is responsible for the uniqueness of each organism.

Base Pairs

Base pairs form the rungs that hold the DNA ladder together. Within a cell, the amount of base A is always equal to the amount of base T, and the amounts of bases G and C are always equal. Use this diagram to explain why this is so.

G

C

T

A

A

T

G

C

DNA Bases

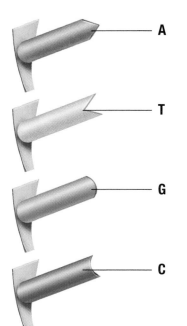

A

T

G

C

Making Copies of DNA

Think about what happens in cell reproduction before mitosis occurs. The chromosomes in the cell's nucleus double, and the DNA in the chromosomes is copied exactly. These exact copies are needed to give each new cell the same instructions that the original cell had.

How is DNA able to make an exact copy of itself? Look at the diagram as you read the following description.

Think of the DNA molecule as a zipper. When you unzip a zipper, the teeth that hold the zipper together separate, and you end up with two halves. The DNA molecule "unzips" when the long strand unwinds and the base pairs separate.

Within each cell nucleus are free-floating bases. These bases are not paired with other bases, but they are

1 *The double strand molecule unzips down the middle as the base pairs separate.*

 2 *Unattached bases float within the nucleus.*

attached to the same molecules that make up the side of the DNA ladder. When the DNA molecule unzips, these bases attach themselves to other bases on the DNA molecule. Remember that bases A and T can fasten only to each other, and G and C can fasten only to each other. This process continues until the two halves of the DNA molecule become two complete double-stranded molecules of DNA. Notice below how each of the two new DNA molecules is identical to the original DNA molecule.

Sections of DNA molecules—genes—direct the building of molecules called proteins. The different cells in your body are largely built from proteins. Your DNA code stores information about what proteins must be made. It also carries instructions that tell the cell when to start or stop building proteins.

4 *The two halves of one DNA molecule become two complete and identical double-strands of DNA.*

3 *Free-floating bases join bases attached to the DNA strands.*

Using DNA Information

High blood pressure

Brown hair color

Green/blue eye color

▲ *Scientists have been able to find the exact location of many traits on the 46 human chromosomes. This drawing of one human chromosome shows just a few.*

Knowledge of DNA has come a long way since Watson and Crick first identified its structure. In 1990, scientists started working on the Human Genome Project. The goal of the project is to locate all the genes on the 46 human chromosomes, as well as to map the sequence of all the base pairs in DNA. The particular order of the bases on the rungs of the DNA ladder is called the DNA sequence. The sequence of DNA in an organism's cells holds the exact genetic instructions needed to make that organism. This complete set of instructions for making an organism is called that organism's genome.

The human genome contains at least 100,000 genes organized into 46 chromosomes. You can see the location of some genes on the chromosome shown to the left.

Since the human genome contains about 3 billion base pairs, the Genome Project is a huge undertaking. Scientists around the world hope to complete the project by the year 2003.

Information from the Human Genome Project and other DNA research may help doctors detect and treat disorders. Scientists have already identified genes that are associated with diseases such as cystic fibrosis and muscular dystrophy. They have also identified genes that seem to make a person more likely to have heart disease, diabetes, and certain cancers.

The fingerprint below is unique to the person who made it. Likewise, each individual has a unique set of

Each person has a set of fingerprints that is unlike that of any other person. The pattern of bands in the DNA "fingerprint" to the right is also unique for each individual. ▼

DNA, which can be used to identify a person. Samples of DNA can be taken from blood, hair, or skin. A special machine analyzes the DNA and produces a characteristic pattern of bands, or a genetic "fingerprint." Why do you think scientists call these patterns a fingerprint?

Police and other law-enforcement workers can use DNA fingerprints to determine whether a suspect was at a crime scene. For example, suppose someone broke into a store and stole some money. While breaking a window, the burglar cut his or her hand on the glass. Blood on the broken window would be an important clue for the police. White blood cells carry a person's DNA. Scientists could analyze the blood and make a DNA fingerprint of the person who broke the window. This fingerprint would be part of the crime evidence gathered.

Suppose the police had three possible suspects in the burglary. They could make a genetic fingerprint of each suspect's DNA. They could then compare the DNA fingerprints of the suspects with the DNA fingerprint collected from the broken, bloody glass at the crime scene. If the bands were to match, the police could be confident they had the right suspect.

The DNA fingerprint to the bottom right is a portion of the fingerprint made from the blood on the store window. Compare it with the DNA fingerprints of the three suspects. Which suspect do you think broke into the store?

Suspect A

Suspect B

Suspect C

Lesson 3 Review

1. Why is every organism unique?

2. Describe the structure of DNA.

3. How does DNA make copies of itself?

4. How is DNA information used?

5. **Metric Conversions**
   A trait of hummingbirds is that they are fast fliers. A hummingbird can fly 80 kilometers per hour. How many centimeters per hour can it fly?

Evidence

▲ The bottom picture represents the DNA fingerprint collected from evidence at the site of the crime. Compare it to the DNA fingerprints above of the three suspects.

Investigating DNA

Process Skills

- estimating and measuring
- observing
- communicating
- inferring

Materials

- safety goggles
- funnel
- graduated plastic cup
- coffee filter
- cup with onion cell mixture
- toothpick with flat end
- meat tenderizer
- rubbing alcohol
- sheet of dark construction paper

Getting Ready

In this activity you will be using an onion cell mixture so that you can see the DNA in an onion cell.

It is easier to see the DNA separate from the onion mixture when the mixture is held against the dark construction paper.

Follow This Procedure

1 Make a chart like the one shown. Use your chart to record your observations.

	Observations
Filtered liquid (step 3)	
Alcohol layer (step 6)	
End of toothpick (step 7)	

2 Put on your safety goggles. Place a funnel in a graduated cup. Fold a coffee filter as shown below. Place the folded filter in the funnel.

3 Pour the cell mixture into the filter paper (Photo A). Allow the liquid portion of the mixture to drip through the filter into the plastic cup until you have collected 60 mL of liquid. Remove the filter and remaining liquid. **Observe** the filtered liquid carefully. Record your observations.

Folding Coffee Filters

1.

2.

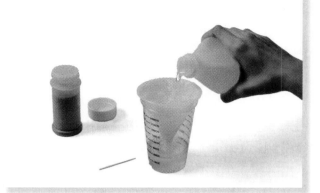

Photo A

④ Using the large end of a flat toothpick, add a few grains of meat tenderizer to the filtered liquid in the cup. Use the toothpick to gently stir the mixture.

⑤ Slowly add rubbing alcohol up to the 120 mL line on the cup. The alcohol will form a layer on top of the onion mixture.

⑥ Place a sheet of dark construction paper behind the cup. Observe the alcohol layer from the side of the cup for several minutes. Record your observations.

⑦ Use a toothpick to slowly stir the alcohol layer. Do not stir the bottom layer. What happens at the end of the toothpick? Record your observations.

Interpret Your Results

1. How did the observations in step 3 compare with those in step 7?

2. The material you collected on the toothpick in step 7 is DNA. Why do you think you were able to see the DNA in step 7 but not in step 3? **Communicate** your ideas to the group.

3. What can you **infer** about the shape of DNA molecules from this activity? Give reasons for your answer.

Inquire Further

How does the DNA of the onion cells you observed compare with the DNA in other organisms? Develop a plan to answer this or other questions you may have.

Self-Assessment

• I followed instructions to isolate DNA from plant cells.

• I recorded my **observations** about what happened as I stirred the alcohol layer.

• I compared the onion cells with the DNA material I collected.

• I **communicated** my ideas about the DNA in step 3 and step 7.

• I made an **inference** about the structure of DNA.

What's the Big Idea?

You will learn:

• how sexual reproduction produces variation in offspring.

• what dominant and recessive genes are.

• how mutations can affect an organism.

How Do Organisms Inherit Traits?

You're looking through an old family photo album. Who's that? He looks just like you! What you're looking at is a picture of your father when he was your age. It's almost **eerie** how much he looks like you. How can that be?

Variation

The members of the family in the picture below look different enough so that you can tell them apart. On the other hand, the children, parents, and grandparents are certainly alike in many ways. For one thing, they all have the traits that you recognize as human traits—two eyes, a nose, a mouth, and two arms, to name just a few.

If you look even more closely at the family, you see that some members share the same shape of nose or the same shape and size of mouth. Children in a family often share

What traits do the children have in common? What traits were passed on to each child from the mother? from the father? from each grandparent? ▶

certain traits with one or both parents. In some cases, children may look more like a grandparent than a parent.

How does a child get his or her mother's eyes or father's nose? The process by which traits are passed from parents to offspring—from generation to generation—is called **heredity**. Remember that genes control how traits develop. When you remember that genes make up chromosomes and that chromosomes are passed on during sexual reproduction, you can begin to see how heredity works.

Recall that DNA in the egg cell combines with DNA in the sperm cell during fertilization. Then a single cell—the zygote—forms. You can see how this happens in the picture to the right.

Find the chromosomes in the sex cells that are alike in size and shape. Each contains genes for similar characteristics. After fertilization, the resulting zygote has a pair of chromosomes that act together to produce traits.

Organisms that are produced as a result of sexual reproduction receive, or **inherit**, at least two genes for every trait. One gene is inherited from the mother. The other gene is inherited from the father.

The children in the picture on page A62 resemble both parents because they inherited chromosomes, and thus genes, from both parents. They each inherited 23 pairs of chromosomes, or a total of 46 chromosomes. One set of 23 chromosomes was inherited from the father. The other set of 23 chromosomes was inherited from the mother.

Not every child in a family receives the same set of genes from the mother and father. Each egg cell of the mother contains a different combination of genes. Each sperm cell of the father also contains a different combination of genes. The appearance of each child in the family results from the particular combinations he or she received during fertilization. So, the children may show differences, or variations, in the same trait. What differences do you see in the children in the family?

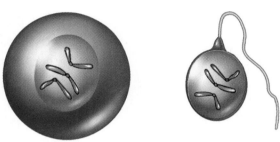

Egg cell   Sperm cell

Fertilization

Zygote

▲ Look closely at the chromosomes in this diagram to see how they form pairs during fertilization.

Glossary

Glossary

dominant gene

(dom′ə nənt jēn), a gene that prevents the expression of another gene

Dominant and Recessive Genes

If you mixed red paint and white paint together, you would expect them to blend to form pink paint. A similar thing happens in some flowers. Plant growers often mix the traits of the same kind of flowers in order to make variations of traits.

For example, a grower can gather pollen from a red flower on a snapdragon plant. The pollen carries genes for red flowers. Then, the grower can brush the pollen onto the pistil of a white flower on a different snapdragon plant. This pistil holds egg cells that carry genes for white flowers. Each new seed that is produced when the pollen fertilizes the eggs will inherit a gene for red flower color and a gene for white flower color. When the seeds are planted, they will grow into new snapdragon plants.

In the new snapdragon plants, the effects of the genes for flower color are blended. Therefore, when the new plants bloom, the flowers will be pink. The diagram shows how this blending occurs. Notice how each flower has a pair of genes that determine its color. The offspring plant received one gene from each parent.

Blending also occurs in some animals. In shorthorn cattle, when a red bull is mated with a white cow, their offspring are roan. Roan calves have a mixture of red and white hairs on their bodies. The same blending occurs when a white bull is mated to a red cow.

The blending effect of the snapdragon genes is only one way genes act together. Many times, two genes do not produce a blended effect. Instead, one trait appears while the other trait stays hidden. In such cases, a **dominant gene** is completely hiding the effect of another gene.

The diagram on the next page shows how flower color is inherited in pea plants. Notice that the offspring pea plant inherited a gene for red flowers from one parent and a gene for white flowers from the other parent. In pea plants, the gene for red flowers is a dominant gene. It is represented by a capital *R*. All dominant traits are represented by capital letters.

Blending of Traits

Compare the offspring produced in this picture with the offspring produced in the picture on the next page. How do they differ? ▼

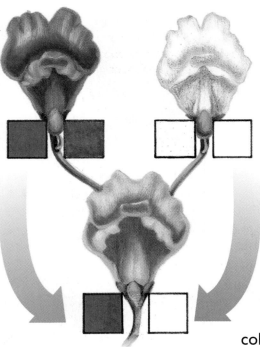

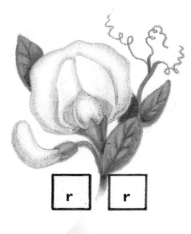

The gene for red flowers hides the effect of the gene for white flowers. The gene whose effect is hidden is called a **recessive gene.** In this case, the gene for white flowers is recessive. It, like all recessive genes, is represented by a small letter.

You might wonder how a pea plant can have white flowers if the gene for red flowers is always dominant. To answer this question, you need to look at the genes of the parents and the offspring. Notice that the parent plant with red flowers has two genes for red flower color. The offspring plant has one gene for red and one gene for white. Because the gene for red flowers is dominant, that plant also has red flowers.

Now look at the parent plant that has white flowers. It has two recessive genes for white flower color. A recessive gene for a trait is expressed only when an organism has two recessive genes for that trait. It must receive a recessive gene from each parent.

An organism with two dominant or two recessive genes for a trait is called **purebred.** Both of the parent pea plants in the diagram are purebred for flower color.

An organism with one dominant and one recessive gene for a trait is a **hybrid.** The offspring pea plant in the diagram is hybrid for flower color. Suppose two pea plants that are hybrid for flower color are bred. What color flowers could their offspring have? The diagram on the right shows you the possible combination of genes for any offspring.

Dominant and Recessive Traits

▲ *These parent pea plants are purebreds. The offspring is a hybrid.*

Glossary

recessive gene
(ri ses′ iv jēn), a gene whose expression is prevented by a dominant gene

purebred (pyür′ bred′), an organism with two dominant or two recessive genes for a trait

hybrid (hī′ brid), an organism with one dominant and one recessive gene for a trait

Glossary

Offspring of Hybrid Plants

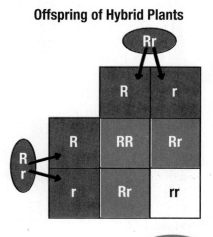

Many traits that you observe in yourself are the result of dominant or recessive traits. Can you roll your tongue like the girl to the left below? If you can, then you have at least one dominant gene for this trait. If you can't, then you must have two recessive genes for the trait. Tongue rolling is only one of the common dominant traits found in humans. Let's look at some others.

Notice the hairline of the girl on the right. Her hairline is straight. Many people have a hairline with a point in the middle of the forehead. This pattern of hair growth is called a widow's peak. This trait is also caused by a dominant gene. If you don't have a widow's peak, you inherited two recessive genes for this trait. If you do, then either your mother or your father—if not both parents— also has a widow's peak.

The boy in the middle has freckles. Freckles are a human trait caused by two recessive genes. How many of your classmates inherited recessive genes for freckles? How many inherited a dominant gene, and thus have no freckles? What about you?

These students are showing some traits. Which of these traits do you have? ▼

Mutations

You learned in Lesson 3 that before a cell divides, each DNA molecule in the cell makes an exact copy of itself. Sometimes during the copying process, mistakes happen. For example, a whole section of the DNA strand might be rearranged so that the base pairs are in a different order. More often, the error is as small as a single base ending up out of place. Any change that occurs when DNA copies itself is a **mutation**.

When a mutation occurs in a sex cell, a different DNA instruction is passed along to the offspring. Some changes in DNA might not change the instructions very much. In such a case, the change might not even be noticed in the offspring. However, other changes can result in the appearance of a new trait.

The bullfrogs to the right blend in well with their environment because of their coloring. They are able to hide from predators. However, the bullfrog below would have a hard time hiding from its enemies. That bullfrog is an albino. The albino bullfrog resulted from a mutation in a gene that causes normal coloring. Its body is not able to make a pigment. Because pigment gives color to skin, the bullfrog is colorless.

Glossary

mutation
(myü tāʹshən), a permanent change in DNA that occurs when DNA copies itself

Glossary

A bullfrog with normal coloring can easily hide along the edge of a pond and snatch up insects. ▼

▲ The mutation that produced this albino frog could have been caused by chemicals or radiation in the environment.

Lesson 4 Review

1. How does sexual reproduction produce variations in offspring?

2. What are dominant and recessive genes?

3. Give an example of how a mutation can affect an organism.

4. **Bar Graphs**
   Survey your class for the trait of eye color. Make a bar graph to show your results.

Investigating Variation in Seedlings

Process Skills

- observing
- predicting
- collecting and interpreting data
- inferring

Materials

- 15 corn seeds
- hand lens
- marker
- masking tape
- aluminum pan
- metric ruler
- seed starter mix
- cup of water
- plastic wrap
- source of light

Getting Ready

In this activity, you'll germinate corn seeds to see if they produce plants that are alike.

Look at the self-assessment section at the end of the activity. This tells you what your teacher will expect of you.

Follow This Procedure

❶ Make a chart like the one shown. Use your chart to record your observations and predictions.

Prediction:			
Date	Seeds germinated	Plants with green leaves	Plants with white leaves

❷ **Observe** some corn seeds with a hand lens. Do you observe any differences? Make a **prediction.** Do you think all the plants grown from these seeds will look alike? Explain why you made the prediction.

❸ Use a marker and masking tape to label an aluminum pan with your group's name. Place about 2 cm of seed starter mix in the bottom of the pan.

❹ Place 15 corn seeds, one by one, in the pan. The seeds should be evenly spaced about 1.5 cm apart (Photo A).

❺ Cover the seeds with a 1 cm layer of starter mix. Gently sprinkle water over the starter mix to make it moist. Cover the pan with plastic wrap and place it in a lighted area (Photo B).

Photo A

Photo B

⑥ Check the seeds each day. If the starter mix starts to dry out, add water to keep it moist.

⑦ Observe when the first seeds begin to germinate. Record the date and the number of seeds germinated. Also record the number of plants with white leaves and the number of plants with green leaves.

⑧ Continue to observe the seeds every other day for 4 more days. Record your observations.

Interpret Your Results

1. What differences did you observe in the dry corn seeds? What differences did you observe in the leaves of the germinated seeds?

2. How does your prediction compare with your results?

3. What **inference** can you make about the presence of chlorophyll and the different colored corn leaves that you observed?

4. What can you infer about the genes of the corn plants you observed?

❓ Inquire Further

Which plants will live longer—the plants with the white leaves or the plants with green leaves? Develop a plan to answer this or other questions you may have.

Self-Assessment

- I followed instructions to germinate corn seedlings.
- I made a **prediction** about how the plants would look.
- I explained why I made the prediction.
- I **collected and interpreted data** about the germinating seeds.
- I made an **inference** about the genes of the corn plants in this activity.

Chapter 2 Review

Chapter Main Ideas

Lesson 1

• Through mitosis and cell division, a cell copies its nucleus to produce two new cells with identical chromosomes.

• Mitosis results in growth and repair.

• In asexual reproduction, two new organisms are produced by just one parent.

Lesson 2

• In meiosis, a cell divides to produce four sex cells, each with half the number of chromosomes as the parent cell.

• In sexual reproduction, an egg cell and a sperm cell join to produce a zygote.

• In mitosis, cells divide once and develop identical offspring. During meiosis, cells divide twice to produce sex cells with half the number of chromosomes as the parent.

Lesson 3

• Organisms are unique because their cells have unique DNA.

• DNA is a coiled strand of base pairs that looks much like a spiraling ladder.

• DNA copies itself when base pairs split and connect with free-floating bases.

• DNA information can be used to treat and identify certain diseases and to identify individuals through their genetic "fingerprint."

Lesson 4

• In sexual reproduction, genes for all traits are inherited from each parent.

• Dominant genes for a trait hide the effect of recessive genes.

• Mutations occur when DNA does not make an exact copy of itself.

Reviewing Science Words and Concepts

Write the letter of the word or phrase that best completes each sentence.

a. asexual reproduction
b. base
c. cell division
d. DNA
e. dominant gene
f. fertilization
g. gene
h. heredity
i. hybrid
j. inherit
k. meiosis
l. mitosis
m. mutation
n. purebred
o. recessive gene
p. sex cell
q. sexual reproduction
r. trait
s. zygote

1. An organism with one dominant and one recessive gene for a trait is a(n) ___.

2. A characteristic of an organism is also called a(n) ___.

3. A(n) ___ hides the effect of a recessive gene.

4. The process that produces cells with half the number of chromosomes as the parent is ___.

5. A molecule that appears in pairs on a DNA strand is a(n) ___.

6. An organism with two dominant or two recessive genes for a trait is a(n) ___.

7. An egg is one kind of ___.

8. Production of new organisms from one parent is ___.

9. A change that occurs in DNA is a(n) ___.

10. The offspring cell formed after fertilization is a(n) ___.

11. The process by which two cells form from one cell is ___.

12. Production of a new organism by two parents is ___.

13. During ___ an egg and sperm cell join.

14. The process that produces new identical nuclei is ___.

15. A substance in chromosomes that directs the cell's activities is ___.

16. The process in which traits pass from parents to offspring is ___.

17. You ___ traits from a parent.

18. A gene whose effect is hidden is a(n) ___.

19. A section of DNA that controls a trait is a(n) ___.

Explaining Science

Use a diagram or write a paragraph to answer these questions.

1. What happens during asexual reproduction of single-cell organisms?

2. What is the role of meiosis and mitosis in sexual reproduction?

3. How does DNA of a chromosome determine an organism's traits?

4. How do offspring inherit traits in sexual reproduction?

Using Skills

1. Make a chart showing the height of each classmate. Show each person's height in millimeters, centimeters, and meters. Decide which **metric** unit is easiest to use to describe height.

2. Suppose you meet a set of identical twins. What can you **infer** about their genes? Give reasons for your inference.

3. **Predict** the possible offspring if two plants are crossed. One plant is purebred with both genes dominant for red flowers. The other is hybrid with genes for red and white flowers.

Critical Thinking

1. Draw and label two diagrams showing the sequence of steps in mitosis and meiosis. Identify the steps in each where a mutation could occur.

2. Suppose you want to breed some plants. You want all the offspring to be the dominant color. Apply what you learned about the way traits are inherited to decide whether the parent plants should be purebred, hybrid, or both.

Don't Mess With Me!

Ouch! Those spines sure are sharp. Wouldn't you want to protect yourself and the water inside your body if you lived outdoors in the harsh conditions of the desert?

Chapter 3
Changing and Adapting

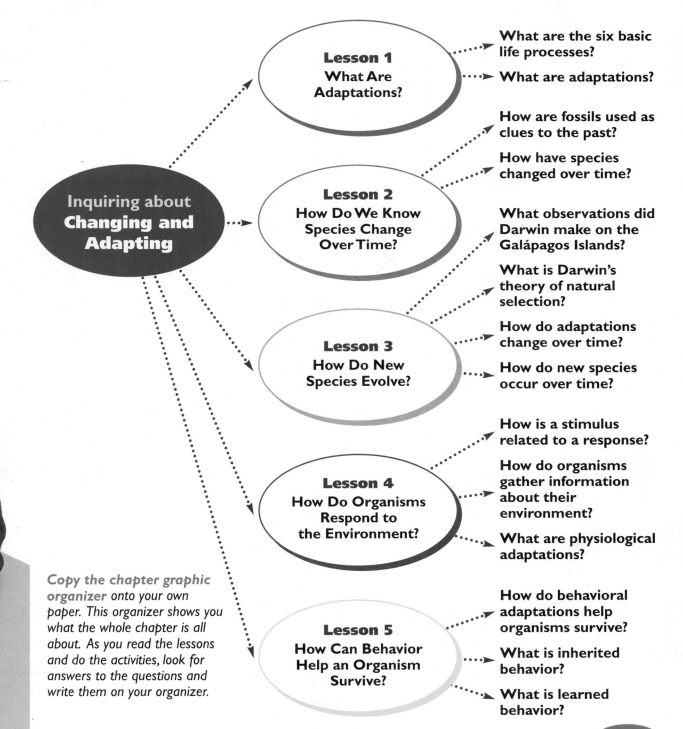

Lesson 1
What Are Adaptations?

What are the six basic life processes?

What are adaptations?

Inquiring about Changing and Adapting

How are fossils used as clues to the past?

How have species changed over time?

Lesson 2
How Do We Know Species Change Over Time?

What observations did Darwin make on the Galápagos Islands?

What is Darwin's theory of natural selection?

How do adaptations change over time?

Lesson 3
How Do New Species Evolve?

How do new species occur over time?

How is a stimulus related to a response?

How do organisms gather information about their environment?

Lesson 4
How Do Organisms Respond to the Environment?

What are physiological adaptations?

How do behavioral adaptations help organisms survive?

Lesson 5
How Can Behavior Help an Organism Survive?

What is inherited behavior?

What is learned behavior?

Copy the chapter graphic organizer onto your own paper. This organizer shows you what the whole chapter is all about. As you read the lessons and do the activities, look for answers to the questions and write them on your organizer.

A73

Exploring Feeding Adaptations

Process Skills

Process Skills

- making a model
- inferring
- communicating

Materials

- envelopes
- model feeding stations
- assorted feeding tools

Explore

1 **Make a model** mouth by placing your hand inside an envelope. Place your thumb at one end of the envelope and your fingers at the other end. Bring the corners of the envelope together to form a beaklike mouth.

2 Look at the model animal feeding stations. You will "adapt" your paper mouth to eat the food at one of the stations. Decide if your model mouth will scoop worms from the ground, grab fish in the sea, or catch bugs in the air.

3 Look at the feeding tools. How could you use them to make a better mouth for catching and eating the food you chose in step 2? Choose a tool—or a combination of tools—and add it to your paper mouth.

4 Go to the feeding station you chose in step 2. Try to catch and eat the food at the station. Can you make your model mouth work better? If so, make changes and try again.

Reflect

1. Communicate your results to your classmates. Based on class results, what can you **infer** about variation in mouth structure and the food an animal eats?

2. Make a list of some other mouth "adaptations" you would like to test.

? Inquire Further

Look at the variety of model mouths your classmates made. Could any of them eat efficiently at all three places? Develop a plan to answer this or other questions you may have.

bugs in air   fish in sea

worms in ground

Drawing Conclusions

Drawing a **conclusion** means using your past experience, previous knowledge, and current information to make a decision or form an opinion. In Lesson 1, *What Are Adaptations?,* you will be drawing conclusions about how adaptations help species survive.

Reading Vocabulary

conclusion, a decision reached by examining all the facts

Example

One way to draw conclusions is to think about past experiences. Make a list of what you already know about the topic. Then think about reasonable explanations for the facts.

When you look at the pictures of the birds and read the text on page A79, think about birds you have observed eating. Use what you already know about the way birds eat to help you draw a conclusion about what each bird eats. For each bird, make a chart of what you already know that might help you draw a conclusion about the bird.

▲ *You can draw conclusions about what each bird eats.*

Talk About It!

1. What have you observed on your own about the way birds eat that might help you to understand what you are reading?

2. What do you observe about each bird's beak that might help you draw conclusions about what kind of food it eats?

You will learn:
- what the six basic life processes are.
- what adaptations are.

What Are Adaptations?

Take a look in the mirror. **Wow!** What human traits do you see? Now picture yourself with a nose like an elephant's trunk and a neck the length of a giraffe's. Would those new traits help or harm you? How?

Life Processes

How do you know that something is alive? You might say that something is alive because it can move. Think about that—a car can move. Does that mean a car is alive? Of course not! You might say that you know you are alive because you can think—but a plant can't think and it's alive. Just how can you tell if something is alive?

Although living things come in many shapes and sizes, like the organisms shown on these pages, they all carry on the same six basic life processes. First, all living things take in energy. They need energy to carry out life processes. An oak tree gets its energy from sunlight. You take in energy by eating food.

Basic Life Processes
Taking in energy
Releasing energy in food
Using energy for body processes
Producing and excreting wastes
Responding to the environment
Reproducing

▲ *This Venus's-flytrap gets nutrients by digesting the insect.*

All living things must release the energy in food in order to use it. To release energy, an organism combines it with oxygen in a process is called respiration. An oak tree, the anteater to the right—and you—all carry on respiration.

Living organisms use the energy that is released from food for growth, movement, repair, and other body processes. A huge oak tree uses energy when it grows from a tiny acorn. The tree also needs energy to repair a wound when a branch is cut off. You, too, use energy for growth and repair. If you cut your finger, your body is able to repair the injury by making new cells. This process uses energy.

Living things must get rid of wastes that are produced during respiration. This process, called excretion, keeps organisms from poisoning themselves with built-up wastes.

Another life process of all living things is reproduction. You learned in Chapter 2 that offspring can be produced from one or two parents. During an oak tree's life, it might produce millions of acorns. Think of the amount of energy that would take! Some of those acorns will grow into oak trees, which produce more acorns.

The beetle in the pictures below is carrying on another life process. The Namib Desert in Africa, where this type of beetle lives, is hot and dry during the day. To escape the heat, the beetles burrow into the sand. In the desert, the beetles don't have any water to drink. However, at night the desert turns misty. Then hundreds of these beetles stand on their heads in long lines along the tops of sand dunes. In the cool air, water collects on the beetles' bodies. As the water collects, it runs down the beetles' bodies into their mouths. The beetles, like all living things, are responding to changes in their environment. If the beetles didn't respond in this way, they couldn't survive in the desert. In what ways do you respond to your environment?

▲ This anteater ingests food, releases the food energy during respiration, and secretes the wastes produced.

Notice the large drop of water at the mouth of this beetle in the top photo. In the bottom photo, you can see how the water collects on the beetle's back. It then runs down the beetle's body to its mouth. ▼

Glossary

adaptation
(ad′ap tā′shən), an inherited trait that helps a species survive in its environment

A beaver has many adaptations that help it survive in its environment. For example, it can hold its breath for 20 minutes or more. How does this adaptation help the beaver survive? ▼

Adaptations

Think of two different species of organisms you are familiar with—perhaps a lion and a tiger. How do they differ from each other? Do you know why they are different? Variations among species are related to survival.

Let's look at some traits of one animal—the beaver—to see how they help it survive. The teeth of a beaver are long and sharp. This trait allows the beaver to chew through tree trunks. With its large, webbed hind feet, a beaver can swim at speeds of 8 kilometers an hour. Its broad, scaly tail helps the beaver steer itself right, left, up, or down. Transparent eyelids cover and protect the beaver's eyes underwater. Long hairs protect its thick undercoat and help it stay warm, even in icy water. A beaver can even close its mouth by pressing flaps of skin behind its front teeth. Then it can chew on wood underwater, without getting water or wood down its throat. These traits help the beavers live successfully in rivers, lakes, and streams.

Where do beavers get these traits? Young beavers inherit all these traits from their parents. An inherited trait that helps a species survive in its environment is an **adaptation.** An adaptation can aid survival in many ways. It might help an organism get food, attract a mate, build a shelter, avoid enemies, or live in a harsh environment.

Bald Eagle

Ruffed Grouse

Pelican

a

b

c

Species do not adapt quickly. Adaptations like those of the beaver take a very long time to develop. Generation after generation reproduces before a trait becomes an adaptation of the entire species.

To get a better understanding of how adaptations help a species survive, look at the pictures on this page. The heads and feet of these birds are mixed up. The head of the bird at the left belongs to a bald eagle. Bald eagles are predators that eat small prey. Which feet might help it catch its prey? The ruffed grouse in the middle lives on the ground. Which feet are best suited for scratching and running? The brown pelican on the right lives on and near the ocean. Which feet might help it swim? How would each bird's survival be affected if it had the mixed-up feet as shown?

▲ *Can you match each bird's head to the correct feet? Each of these birds eats a different kind of food. Which pair of feet would help each bird with its task of catching food?*

Lesson 1 Review

1. What are the six basic life processes?

2. What are adaptations?

3. **Draw Conclusions**
   Suppose a friend shows you an interesting object under a microscope and tells you it is a living organism. What conclusions can you draw about the organism?

What's the Big Idea?

You will learn:

- how fossils are used as clues to the past.
- how species have changed over time.

How Do We Know Species Change Over Time?

Zap! You're in a time machine that has taken you back 65 million years. What do you see? You might watch a tiny dinosaur hatching from an egg. You'd better take photos. How else will people know what life was like so long ago?

Fossils—Clues to the Past

You know that time machines don't exist, so how do scientists know what life was like on Earth long, long ago? One way that scientists learn about the different kinds of organisms that have lived on Earth is by studying fossils. Fossils are the remains or traces of organisms that once lived. They are a record of past life on Earth. Look at the pictures on these two pages to see some different kinds of fossils.

Many fossils form when organisms die and sink to the bottom of a stream, ocean, or swamp. There, the organisms are covered by sediment—mud, sand, or clay that settles to the bottom of the water. Over millions of years, the sediment changes to rock. The remains of the organisms in the rock layers are fossils. Even the burrows of worms and other animals, termite nests, and animal droppings have been found as fossils.

Most often, an organism's hard parts, such as its shell, bones, or teeth, are the only body parts that become fossils. Soft body parts usually decay without leaving a trace.

However, in the 1980s, an Italian fossil hunter found an unusual specimen. He

Some of the most common fossils are molds of the shells of ammonites. The soft body parts of these organisms were not fossilized. The shells range in size from 13 centimeters to 2 meters. ▼

thought that the fossil was a bird. Later in the 1990s, paleontologists—scientists who study fossils—examined the fossil. They realized that it belonged to a 110-million-year-old baby dinosaur. The unusual thing about the fossil was that some of the dinosaur's soft tissue also fossilized along with the bones. Scientists were able to see parts of a dinosaur that they had never seen before—most of its intestines and muscles, the windpipe, and perhaps the liver.

The lungs of the dinosaur were not fossilized. However, by studying the position of the intestines, researchers might be able to figure out the size and the shape of the lungs. With this information they can come closer to answering an important question—Were dinosaurs more closely related to reptiles or to birds?

Scientists have found nearly complete fossils of other kinds of organisms. The insects below were trapped when the sticky resin of an ancient pine tree flowed over it. Later, the tree resin hardened into what we call amber, and the insect was fossilized. Plant seeds, feathers, and even frogs have been found preserved in amber.

When scientists find fossils, they combine new information from the fossils with what they already know to draw conclusions about life long, long ago. New evidence can help support what scientists believe to be true, or at times the new evidence will prove scientists wrong. Each new piece of information helps scientists form a better picture of life that no one has seen.

▲ Notice that the fossil dragonfly at the top looks similar to the one directly below it, which lives today. Today's dragonflies are large insects with wingspans up to 14 centimeters. However, dragonflies that lived 250 million years ago had a wingspan of up to 80 cm!

Much amber, like what you see here, is found in Europe along the shores of the Baltic Sea, where it formed 40 to 60 million years ago. Organisms like these insects were often trapped in the amber. ▶

Glossary

evolution (ev′ə lü shən), process that results in changes in the genetic makeup of a species over very long periods

Change Over Time

Recall from Chapter 2 that mutations are changes in an organism's DNA. Some mutations lead to traits that harm an individual—like the albino frog you learned about in Chapter 2. Other mutations lead to traits that are helpful. Harmful mutations could cause an organism to die, but organisms with helpful mutations may produce offspring with similar traits. These traits, in turn, can be passed from generation to generation for many years.

When helpful mutations are passed along to future generations, a species' chances of survival improve. Genetic change that occurs within a species over long periods, from generation to generation, is called **evolution**. What evidence do scientists have that organisms evolve?

You've learned that fossils give scientists clues to past life on Earth. Usually, the fossil record is incomplete. Working with an incomplete fossil record is like working with a jigsaw puzzle that has some missing pieces. You can still figure out the whole puzzle picture when only a few pieces are missing. Likewise, scientists can use fossil "puzzle pieces" to determine what the whole picture is. Often, fossil puzzle pieces indicate to scientists how certain species evolved over time.

Evolution of the Camel

By studying fossil bones, scientists have been able to put the pieces together to show the evolution of the common camel. ▼

65 million years ago   54 million years ago   37 million years ago

Scientists have used fossil puzzle pieces to conclude how today's camel evolved over millions of years. The pictures at the bottom of these pages show some of the steps in the camel's evolution. Scientists have studied the fossil leg bones, skulls, and teeth of different camel species that have lived over a period of 65 million years. These fossils indicate that the first camels were small animals the size of a rabbit. What evidence do you think scientists used to form this conclusion?

Fossils indicate that by 37 million years ago, camels still had a small body size, feet with four toes, and teeth with low crowns. Crowns are the part of the teeth that show above the gums. Over time, camels appear to have evolved into larger animals.

By 26 million years ago, the larger camel species had feet with only two toes and teeth with high crowns. Its hump began to appear. What other difference do you notice in the camel during this 65-million-year period?

Lesson 2 Review

1. How are fossils used as clues to the past?

2. Give an example of how species have changed over time.

3. **Draw Conclusions**
   Look at the insects trapped in the amber on page A81. What conclusion can you draw about these insects?

26 million years ago   **Present time**

What's the Big Idea?

You will learn:

- what observations Charles Darwin made on the Galápagos Islands.
- what Darwin's theory of natural selection is.
- how adaptations change over time.
- how new species occur over time.

The HMS Beagle traveled around the world. Its most important stop was at the Galápagos Islands, where Darwin made observations that led to an understanding of how species evolve. ▼

Lesson 3

How Do New Species Evolve?

Hey! Look at that weird insect. What does it do with those strange pinchers on its body? And those eyes. They look so huge! Why does an insect need these strange looking body parts? How did it get them in the first place?

Charles Darwin

History of Science

On December 27, 1831, the ship HMS *Beagle* sailed from England to study the coast of South America. It was on this ship that some important ideas about how species evolve began to develop. You can follow the course of the *Beagle* on the map.

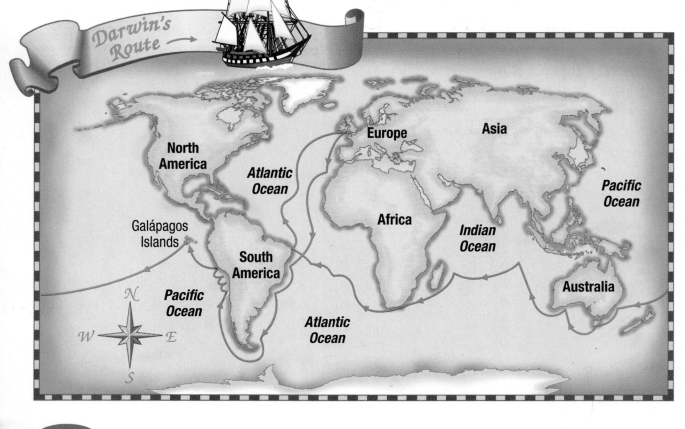

Darwin's Route →

North America

Atlantic Ocean

Galápagos Islands

South America

Pacific Ocean

Europe

Asia

Africa

Indian Ocean

Pacific Ocean

Australia

Atlantic Ocean

N
W   E
S

On board the *Beagle* was 22-year-old Charles Darwin. As the ship's naturalist, Darwin's job was to collect and describe the many different species he observed at the places the ship visited. When Darwin left for the trip, he was convinced that species didn't change. In 1835, the *Beagle* reached the Galápagos Islands after making stops on the continent of South America. The Galápagos Islands were named after the Spanish word for *tortoise* because of the giant land tortoises found living on them. Find these islands on the map.

For five weeks, Darwin roamed the Galápagos Islands. He made many observations and collected many specimens. The observations that Darwin made on the islands later changed his view about species.

Darwin found many unusual species living on the islands. Many of these species weren't found anywhere else in the world. Although many resembled species that Darwin had seen in other places, each species was different from every other species in some way.

For example, Darwin discovered that island inhabitants could tell what island a tortoise came from just by looking at it. One clue was the color of the tortoise's shell. Another clue was its shape. The two main shapes of shells depended on the kind of island where the tortoise lived. On the one hand, one island had humid, green highlands with many short plants. Tortoises on this and similar islands had dome-shaped shells, short necks, and short front legs, as in the upper picture. These tortoises were adapted to eating ground plants.

Tortoises from low, dry islands looked more like the tortoise in the lower picture. They were smaller and had long necks and slender legs. The front parts of the tortoises' shells were bent upward in the shape of a saddle. This shell shape made it possible for the tortoise to reach high into the dry shrubs to feed.

▲ The differences in shape of the shells of these two tortoises give clues to the kind of environment in which they live. What other differences can you observe?

Glossary

natural selection
(nach′ər əl si lek′shən),
the idea that those
organisms best adapted to
their environment will be
the ones most likely to
survive and reproduce

Darwin noticed that tortoises weren't the only animals that differed from island to island. He observed at least 13 different species of finches. The finches resembled those he had seen on the continent. Darwin thought that perhaps finches from the continent had landed on the island and produced offspring. Then Darwin noticed that the species on each island had different kinds of beaks that seemed to match the kinds of food they ate. For example, some finches had long beaks for removing insects hidden deep within a tree's bark. Others had short, thick beaks for cracking nuts. Darwin recorded his thoughts about these differences by writing that "one might really fancy that one species had been modified for different ends."

Natural Selection

History of Science

Darwin returned from his trip on the *Beagle* in 1836. He spent the next 20 years studying his specimens, conducting experiments, analyzing his observations, and developing his ideas about how species evolve. During that time, Darwin thought about a common practice used by farmers. The process, called selective breeding, involves breeding only plants or animals that have desired traits. For example, sheep farmers often kept only the sheep with the best wool to be parents of their future flocks. After several generations, the offspring would have much thicker wool than even the original parents. Darwin wondered if some type of selective breeding occurred in nature. In other words, did nature select certain traits over others?

After nearly 20 years of study, Darwin theorized that, indeed, nature did select certain traits over others. He proposed the theory of evolution by **natural selection**. Darwin's ideas are summarized on the next page.

Charles Darwin is the founder of the modern theory of evolution. ▼

Main Points of Darwin's Theory

1 **Organisms usually produce more offspring than can survive.**
Female frogs lay large clusters of eggs in the water of a pond. Individual egg clusters range from a few eggs to hundreds of eggs. A female bullfrog may lay as many as 20,000 eggs. Only a few eggs will survive to become adult frogs.

2 **Competition exists among organisms. Those organisms that survive the competition are the only ones to reproduce and pass on their traits to offspring.**
Adult male elephants often fight to test their strength. Only the strongest bulls mate with females to produce offspring.

3 **Organisms best adapted to their environments are the ones most likely to survive long enough to reproduce.**
Desert plants compete for a limited amount of water. Having a waxy skin and spines rather than leaves reduces the amount of water a cactus loses. These adaptations allow cacti to survive in the desert.

4 **Parent organisms pass traits on to their offspring. Offspring usually look like their parents, but variations may occur.**
These tree snails are members of the same species, but they have shells that vary in color. The color variations of these snails will be passed on to their offspring.

Glossary

structural adaptation
(struk′chər əl ad′ap tā′
shən), adaptation that
involves body parts or
color

Adaptations Over Time

You've seen how some traits help a particular organism survive in its environment better than other organisms of the same species without the traits. These traits that enable an organism to survive are passed from generation to generation. Over time, more and more members of the species share these traits. Eventually, these traits may become adaptations of the species.

The mole rat shown on the next page is a good example of how adaptations evolve. Today mole rats live underground. They use their long front teeth and claws to help dig tunnels. Their tiny eyes don't see well. They don't need to—it's dark where they live! Mole rats feel their way around in their dark tunnels with sensitive hairs on their heads. These traits that make mole rats well suited to live in their environment are examples of structural adaptations. **Structural adaptations** are any coloring or body parts that help an organism survive.

How did these structural adaptations evolve in mole rats? The pictures below give you one explanation that scientists have developed.

Evolution of the Mole Rat

▲ *The ancestors of mole rats lived aboveground and had different traits from those of today's mole rats.*

▲ *Over time, variation in structural adaptations occurred. For example, larger teeth and claws helped some individuals dig underground. They were safer from predators. These variations were passed on to offspring.*

Often structural adaptations take thousands or even millions of years to evolve. However, sometimes they occur in a population more quickly. The peppered moths shown to the right are a good example of rapid evolution.

Until the 1850s, almost all peppered moths in England were pale speckled gray. Dark gray peppered moths were so rare that they were prized by moth collectors.

Around 1850, dark moths started to become more common, especially near cities where factories were located. The increase in dark moths occurred at the same time that more and more factories were being built. Light tree trunks in those areas became darkened with soot from the factory smokestacks. Dark moths sitting on soot-darkened trees blended in and were harder for birds to see than light moths. Thus, they were more likely to escape being eaten by birds. They survived and passed on genes for dark color to their offspring.

However, in the countryside, the situation didn't change. There, the trees were not darkened by pollution from factories. On the light-barked trees, dark moths were easier for hungry birds to spot. Most of the peppered moths continued to be light colored.

▲ Peppered moths exist in two varieties—dark and light. Which moth blends in better with this light tree bark? Which moth would more likely be noticed by a hungry bird and eaten?

▲ Over many generations, evolution resulted in the adaptations of today's mole rats.

New Species over Time

You've seen how adaptations evolve within a species, but how do new species evolve? Look at the drawings on these two pages. Suppose a group of frogs of the same species— a **population**—lives near a small stream as in picture 1. This population of frogs has slight variations in color. Some are dark and some are light. At first, the stream is small enough that the frogs can cross the stream to mate. The offspring that are produced by these frogs share the same traits as the parents share.

What would happen if, as in pictures 2 and 3, the stream became wider and flowed more rapidly over time? A large canyon might form. The frog population on one side of the canyon would become isolated from the population on the other side because they wouldn't be able to cross the canyon. Frogs from one side would no longer be able to mate with frogs from the other side.

What might result from this isolation? At first, the frogs from each population would share the same traits. But the conditions on each side of the canyon might vary in some ways. For example, the vegetation on the two sides might vary. Each population of frogs would adapt to the environment it lives in through the process of natural selection. In time, the frogs from one side of the canyon

When a population is divided and one group becomes isolated from the other in a different environment, a new species may evolve. ▼

▲ How do these two species of frogs differ? How is each species adapted to its environment?

would become different enough from the population of frogs on the other side to form two different species. Each species would be adapted to a slightly different environment.

Sometimes isolation occurs because animals migrate. This is what happened on the Galápagos Islands. Animals from Central and South America flew, swam, or were carried on clumps of dirt or plants to the islands. When these populations were cut off from one another, they adapted to their new environment and evolved into separate species.

Lesson 3 Review

1. What observations did Darwin make on the Galápagos Islands?

2. What is Darwin's theory of natural selection?

3. How do adaptations change over time?

4. How do new species occur over time?

5. **Draw Conclusions**
   What conclusions did Darwin draw about the differences in the beaks of different species of finches on the Galápagos Islands?

What's the Big Idea?

You will learn:

- how a stimulus is related to a response.
- how organisms gather information about their environment.
- what physiological adaptations are.

Glossary

Glossary

stimulus (stim′yə ləs), a change in the environment of an organism that causes a response

response (ri spons′), a reaction of an organism to a change in the environment

Ptarmigan in Winter

▲ The color change of the ptarmigan is an inherited trait that improves its chances of survival in its environment. ▶

Lesson 4

How Do Organisms Respond to the Environment?

You're outside, shooting hoops. Suddenly the wind starts to blow, and the temperature drops. **Brrr!** You start to shiver. You grab a jacket. You are reacting to a change in your environment.

Stimulus and Response

You've read about how evolution produces species that are adapted to their environment. An important adaptation for any organism is the way it reacts to changes within its environment. Look at the ptarmigan in the photos. What kind of change in its environment causes the change you see?

The change in environment that causes the reaction is called a **stimulus**. The reaction—a change in color—is called a **response**. All organisms have stimulus-and-response reactions. The response of the ptarmigan is so extreme that you may think you are seeing two different birds. In far northern Canada and Alaska where

ptarmigans live, summers are short and cool. The bird's feathers are flecked brown. This coloring allows it to blend well with its brown and green surroundings.

Ptarmigan in Summer

However, when early snows start to cover the ground, the white feathers of the ptarmigan gradually replace the brown ones. By the time the environment is completely snow covered, the ptarmigan is totally white. The new color helps the bird survive in its winter environment.

Have you ever played basketball like the girls in the pictures? The girl on the right is responding to an external stimulus—a stimulus from outside the body. What is this external stimulus? When you eat pizza because you are hungry or drink lemonade because you are thirsty, you are responding to internal stimuli—stimuli from inside the body—hunger and thirst.

▲ Stimulus-and-response reactions play an important role in this basketball game.

Plants, too, respond to stimuli. You may have noticed how the stems and leaves of a houseplant on a window ledge curve toward sunlight. This response happens because plants respond to light by growing toward it. Some plants open or close their flowers in response to changes in light or temperature. The leaves of the Venus's-flytrap on page A76 respond to the touch of an insect by snapping shut.

Remember that response is a basic life process. Even single-celled organisms respond to their environment. For example, some bacteria respond to a lack of water by forming a new, thick membrane inside the old one. The cell material outside the new membrane dies. The organism is then called a bacterial spore. The spore can remain inactive until water is in the bacteria's environment again.

Gathering Information About the Environment

In order for an organism to respond successfully to changes in its environment, it first must get information about those changes. Compare the different ways the organisms on these two pages gather this information.

Sharks

▲ Sharks have eyes that see well in dim light. Their nostrils are excellent at sensing the smell of blood in the water. Tiny scale-covered openings on their sides detect vibrations in the water. Also, structures on their snout pick up weak electrical signals given off by muscle contractions of other organisms.

Snakes

◀ Snakes use their tongues and a special organ in the roof of the mouth to pick up the body scent of animals. Some snakes have heat receptors along the upper margins of the lips. Others have a pair of organs at the front of the head that allow the snake to detect heat from its prey.

Flies

◀ *Flies taste with hairs around their mouths. They also taste with their feet. That's why you might see a fly walking across your food. It's testing the taste! Flies also have sensors for touch and temperature on their legs. The eyes of a fly don't form clear images, but they can easily detect movement.*

Moths

▲ *Male moths use sensory hairs on their feathery antennae to detect chemicals produced by female moths. These detectors enable them to find females during mating season. Some moth species can detect these chemicals more than a kilometer away.*

Squid

◀ *Squid use their large eyes to find prey and avoid danger in dark ocean waters. The eyes of a squid can form real images, just as your eyes do. Because of this ability, squids can judge distance accurately.*

Glossary

physiological adaptation

(fiz′ē ə loj′ə kəl ad′ap tā′shən), adaptation that involves a body part's job of controlling a life process

Plant Leaf

This photo shows a magnified image of the outer layer of a leaf. Notice the pores that allow important gases to enter and leave the cell. The guard cells control the opening and closing of the pores. ▼

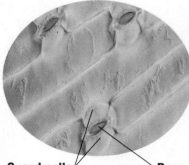

Guard cells   **Pore**

Physiological Adaptations

For plants to survive, carbon dioxide must enter the leaves, and water vapor and oxygen must exit. The tiny pores you see in the leaf cells to the left below open and close to control the flow of these and other gases. Each pore is surrounded by two special guard cells. During the day, water moves into the guard cells, causing them to swell and bend. The pore opens. At night the guard cells lose water into surrounding cells, causing them to straighten, and the pore closes. The guard cells are able to do this because of a **physiological adaptation**—an adaptation in which an organism's body part does its job in response to a stimulus.

Like all sea mammals, the seal shown below must swim to the surface of the water to breathe. It holds its breath while underwater, searching for food. In fact, some seals can hold their breath for as long as an hour.

In the case of the seal, the stimulus is the lower amount of oxygen that gets into its blood when it hold its breath. What is the seal's response? The seal's response is to "shut off" the blood circulation in the outer layers of its body and limbs. This response conserves oxygen, so the seal doesn't have to breathe as often. A physiological adaptation enables the seal to respond in this way.

◀ *This seal feeds on fish, squid, krill, and seabirds that it catches while swimming. Holding its breath while swimming underwater is one response of the seal to its environment. What others can you think of?*

Sweaty socks are just one result of some physiological adaptations you have. When you are very active, such as during a basketball game, your muscles produce a lot of heat energy. To keep from overheating, your body reacts in several ways. For one thing, blood vessels in your skin enlarge. As more blood flows through the vessels, more heat is carried to your body's surface. The heat escapes through your skin. Also, your sweat glands become more active. When the sweat evaporates from your skin, it cools your body. In other words, your body senses a change in internal temperature and responds to it.

▲ Single-celled organisms like this ameba respond to changes in their environments.

The ameba at the top of the page has physiological adaptations that allow it to respond to light and certain materials that are found in the water surrounding its body. The mimosa plant shown here has adaptations that allow it to respond to the external stimulus of the person's touch. Its leaves close and droop. The plant's response is due to the quick loss of water from special cells at the base of each leaf. What other responses do organisms have to their external environment?

Lesson 4 Review

1. How is a stimulus related to a response?

2. What are two ways that organisms gather information about their environment?

3. What are physiological adaptations?

4. **Draw Conclusions**
   Look at the photo of the plant leaf on page A96. Was the photo most likely taken during the day or at night? Give the reasons for your conclusion.

▲ The response of the mimosa plant to touch is to close its leaves. Scientists think this response protects the plant by conserving water and by making it look less tasty to insects and other animals.

Observing the Effects of Salt Water on Cells

Process Skills

- observing
- communicating
- inferring

Materials

- piece of red onion
- forceps
- microscope slide with coverslip
- dropper
- water
- microscope
- salt solution
- paper towel

Getting Ready

Fresh water plants can't survive in salt water. Do this activity to find out why.

You might want to practice tearing small pieces of onion until you can get a piece with a thin red layer.

Review the proper use of a microscope.

Follow This Procedure

1 Make a chart like the one shown. Use your chart to record your observations.

Cells in water	Cells in salt water

2 Gently and slowly bend a small piece of red onion until it breaks in half. Look for a thin layer of red tissue at the edge of the tear (Photo A). Remove this thin layer, being careful not to wrinkle it.

3 Use forceps to place the thin piece of onion on a microscope slide. Use the dropper to add one or two drops of water to the slide. Place a coverslip over the onion skin.

4 Place the slide on the microscope stage. Carefully turn the adjustment knob of the microscope to focus on several onion cells. Observe the cells. Draw what you see.

Self-Monitoring

Was I careful to focus the lens away from the microscope slide?

Photo A

Photo B

Photo C

5 Remove the slide from the microscope stage. Using a dropper, place a drop of the salt solution along the right edge of the coverslip (Photo B).

6 Place a small piece of paper towel in the forceps. Touch the paper towel along the left edge of the coverslip. This will draw the salt solution under the coverslip. Repeat this step so that there are two drops of salt water under the coverslip (Photo C).

7 Place the slide back on the microscope stage. Observe the cells for about 3 minutes. Make a sketch of what you see.

Interpret Your Results

1. Look at your drawings of the onion cells before and after the salt water was added. **Communicate** how the cells are alike and how they are different.

2. Draw a conclusion. Are onion cells adapted to salt water? What observations support your conclusion?

3. Make an **inference.** What would happen if you introduced a salt water solution to animal cells?

Inquire Further

How do animal cells react in the presence of salt water? Develop a plan to answer this or other questions you may have.

> ### Self-Assessment
>
> - I followed instructions to test the effects of salt water on plant cells.
> - I made **observations** of the plant cells in water and in the salt water solution.
> - I **communicated** by drawing what I saw when I looked at the onion cells through the microscope.
> - I drew a conclusion about onion cells and salt water.
> - I made an **inference** about how salt water might affect animal cells.

You will learn:
- how behavioral responses help organisms survive.
- what inherited behavior is.
- what learned behavior is.

This Ringed plover is pretending to be injured in order to distract a predator from its nest. This is a behavioral adaptation. ▼

Lesson 5

How Can Behavior Help an Organism Survive?

Zzzz! Have you ever pretended to be asleep when you really weren't? If so, you might say you "played possum." The act gets its name from the way an opossum sometimes behaves. Playing possum can save an opossum's life.

Behavioral Adaptations

Behavior is one kind of response an organism can make to a stimulus. An organism's behavior includes all the actions of that organism. What are some of your behaviors?

Some behaviors help animals escape danger. Other behaviors help adults protect their young. The Ringed plover in the picture is protecting its young by pretending to have a broken wing. Although it risks its own life, the adult's display may draw the attention of the predator away from the young in the nest. In this way, the young have a better chance of survival. When the danger is gone, the plover returns to its nest. This unusual response of the plover is a **behavioral adaptation**.

The behavioral adaptations of the plover help individual organisms survive. Sometimes, behavioral adaptations help an entire population survive. Termites are an example. Look at the termite colony to the right.

Four different kinds of termites within the same species share a termite mound. Each kind of termite has different behaviors that aid the survival of the colony. Worker termites gather food, care for offspring, and build the tunnels and chambers of the mound. Soldier termites guard the tunnels and covered trails that extend out from the nest. A single queen termite lays all the eggs, and a king termite fertilizes all the eggs.

Behavioral adaptations also help organisms get food. A spider spins a web in which to capture flying insects.

Still other behavioral adaptations help animals, such as the crocodile, find mates. A male crocodile swims to a female and strokes her with his head and front legs. After mating, the female builds a mounded nest on land and protects her eggs. After the eggs hatch, she continues to care for her young. She may even carry them through the water in her mouth, as you see in the picture. A female cares for her young for up to a year.

How do crocodiles get these behaviors? An organism's behavior can result from the species's adaptations or from learning. The crocodile's behaviors probably are the result of adaptations that it inherited from its parents.

▲ Few reptiles show as much gentle care for their young as a mother crocodile. Young crocodiles are often killed by predators. To protect them, the mother carries them to safety!

◄ A termite mound can house up to 5 million insects, but only one queen. The large termite in the center is the queen.

Glossary

instinct (in′stingkt), an inherited behavior

Inherited Behavior

A behavior that an organism is born with is an inherited behavior. Inherited behavior is a way of responding to a stimulus that doesn't require learning.

One type of inherited behavior is an **instinct**. All young are born with instincts. For example, the behavior of the newly hatched kittiwakes in the photo results from instincts. Notice that the birds nest on high cliffs. When young kittiwakes hatch, they instinctively remain still in the nest. If they moved around, they could fall off the cliff. The young of ground-nesting birds do not show this same instinctive behavior. Their young move around soon after they hatch.

Not all instinctive behavior is simple. Some instinctive behavior may involve several steps and take several weeks to complete. For example, brown-headed cowbirds don't build nests. When the female is ready to lay eggs, she scouts the area to locate the nests of other birds. She finds the nest of another species where the female is laying eggs. She waits quietly until the other female flies off to feed. Then the cowbird moves in and quickly lays a single egg among the other eggs in the nest. Every morning for four or five days, the cowbird lays an egg in a different nest. Then she leaves. The female birds who laid the other eggs in the nests incubate the cowbird's egg along with their own.

◀ *Large colonies of kittiwakes nest high on cliffs.*

Glossary

instinct (in′stingkt), an inherited behavior

Another example of instinctive behavior is web spinning. Have you ever watched a spider spin a web like the one in the picture? It's a complex process. Yet spiders spin webs correctly the very first time. The kind of web a spider spins is an inherited behavior. For example, an orb weaver spider does not spin the same kind of web as a cobweb weaver spider.

The simplest inherited behavior is a **reflex.** A reflex is a quick automatic response to a stimulus. In a reflex, a signal passes from a sense organ, such as your eye, along nerves to your spinal cord and right back to your muscles. The message doesn't have to travel to the brain for a reaction to occur. A reflex occurs very quickly—in less than a second. It happens without an organism's thinking about it. For example, if something is thrown toward your face, you blink your eyes as shown below. If you touch a hot stove or a sharp thorn, you jerk your hand away. Or, if something irritates your nose, you sneeze.

All animals have reflexes. The fur on a cat's back stands on end when it is frightened. An octopus changes color when it senses danger. When a light is turned on, a cockroach runs from it. If you swat at a fly, it flies away. Reflexes allow an animal to act quickly, especially in times of danger.

Glossary

reflex (rē′fleks), quick, automatic response to a stimulus

Glossary

▲ This garden spider is born with instincts that enable it to spin this web. What instincts were you born with?

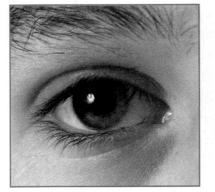
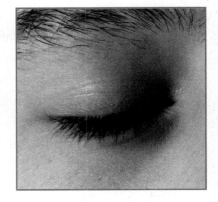

Blinking Reflex
◄ Your eye blinks reflexively whenever an object quickly approaches your face. How does this reflex help protect you?

Learned Behavior

Can you remember when you learned to ride a bicycle, roller-skate, or hit a softball? You probably fell several times while trying to balance on a bike or skates. You probably missed hitting the ball a lot at first. But eventually you learned to do these things without having to think about them.

Many animal behaviors are learned. Think about very young leopard cubs. They are quite helpless when they are first born. Their mother cares for them and nurses them. When the cubs are older, the mother will lead them to an animal she has killed. They start eating solid food. The young leopards spend about two years with their mother learning to hunt. At first, they mostly watch what their mother does. Later, they begin to hunt with her. Finally, when they are fully grown and can hunt well enough, the cubs go off on their own.

A trained guide dog helps a blind person get around without danger. What might a dog trained to help a deaf person need to learn? ▼

If you have a dog, you may have observed some learned behavior. A dog usually learns to come when its name is called. It may have learned to sit or stay when told. Some animals come running when they hear the sound of an electric can opener. They have learned that the sound may mean dinner is about to be served. Goldfish who are fed by people learn to come to the surface of a pond. They come when people stand by the pond, even if there's no food.

The dog in the photo was trained as a guide dog. When the dog was about a year old, it began its training. It had to learn to obey commands and to take a person safely through crowds, traffic, and other hazards, such as this forest. The dog had to learn to disobey commands that might put its owner in danger. Finally, when the dog is fully trained, it begins work as a guide dog.

You may have seen young ducklings like the ones below following their mother. Within a short time after hatching, ducklings follow the first moving object they see. If that object is the mother duck, they follow her. This behavior is important because they then learn to watch her and do what she does. They learn to find food and escape predators.

However, ducklings hatched in an incubator may see a human as the first moving object. They follow the human. In this case, the human must teach the ducklings how to behave in order to survive. They must learn to go to water to swim and get food. Fortunately for ducklings, swimming is not a learned behavior.

Imprinting
▲ These baby mallard ducks will follow the first moving object they see when they hatch. This behavior is called imprinting.

Lesson 5 Review

1. How do behavioral adaptations help an organism survive?

2. What is inherited behavior?

3. What is learned behavior?

4. **Draw Conclusions**
   A human infant learns to walk at about one year. Is this behavior learned or inherited? Give reasons for your conclusion.

Investigating How Plants React to Light

Process Skills

Process Skills

- predicting
- observing
- communicating
- inferring

Materials

- large shoe box with lid
- small bean plant
- marker
- scissors
- pieces of cardboard
- masking tape
- light source

Getting Ready

In this activity, you will find out how light can affect a plant's growth.

As part of this activity, you will create a maze. It might be helpful to first look up or study some simple mazes—perhaps in a puzzle book.

Follow This Procedure

1 Make a chart like the one shown. Use your chart to record your observations.

Day	Observations
2	
4	
6	
8	
10	

2 Stand a shoe box on one of its ends. Place a small bean plant inside the shoe box. Use a marker to make a line inside the box to show the height of the plant (Photo A).

3 Remove the plant from the box.

4 Cut an opening about 4 cm wide at the end of the box opposite where the plant will be placed. This hole will be the light source for the plant (Photo A).

5 Draw a maze inside the shoe box. You might use a design like the one shown in Photo A, or make one of your own. Be sure to allow room at the bottom of the box for the plant. Secure a piece of cardboard to the shoe box with masking tape to make the first wall of the maze (Photo B).

Photo A

Photo B

6 Mark one side of the plant pot with an X. Place your plant inside the box with the X facing the back of the box.

7 Place the lid on the box. Place the box under a light source. **Predict** how the plant will grow. Give reasons for your prediction.

8 **Observe** the plant every 2 days and record what you observe about its growth. As the plant grows above the first wall, add the next wall to your maze. Be sure to water the plant when necessary. If you take the plant out of the box, use the X to make sure you place the plant back in the same position.

9 Repeat step 8 for all of the walls that you have.

Interpret Your Results

1. Use your observations to **communicate** to the class how the barriers in the box affected the plant's growth.

2. Why do you think the plant grew the way it did?

3. Make an **inference.** What would happen if you added more walls to your maze? How might the plant's growth be affected?

Inquire Further

How would the plant's growth be affected if you added more walls to your maze? Develop a plan to answer this or other questions you may have.

Self-Assessment

- I followed instructions to test how a plant reacts to light.
- I **predicted** how the plant would grow.
- I recorded my **observations** about the plant's growth.
- I used my observations to **communicate** about why the plant grew as it did.
- I made an **inference** about how the height of the barriers might affect the plant's growth.

Chapter 3 Review

Chapter Main Ideas

Lesson 1
• All living things take in energy, release energy in food, use energy, excrete wastes, reproduce, and respond to the environment.
• Adaptations are inherited traits that help a species survive.

Lesson 2
• Fossils give clues about the organisms that lived long ago.
• Species have changed as a result of evolution.

Lesson 3
• Darwin discovered that species are adapted to their different environments.
• Darwin's theory of natural selection states that certain traits are selected over others and organisms best suited to their environment will survive.
• Adaptations that enable an organism to survive are passed on to offspring.
• Sometimes new species evolve when populations are isolated.

Lesson 4
• A stimulus is a change in environment that causes a response or reaction.
• Organisms use sensory organs to gather information about their environment.
• Physiological adaptations are the work of body parts in response to stimuli.

Lesson 5
• Behavior adaptations cause actions that enable organisms to survive.
• Inherited behavior is a way of responding that does not require learning.
• Learned behavior is an action that is not inherited from the parents.

Reviewing Science Words and Concepts

Choose the letter of the answer that best matches each description.

a. adaptation
b. behavioral adaptation
c. evolution
d. instinct
e. natural selection
f. physiological adaptation
g. population
h. reflex
i. response
j. stimulus
k. structural adaptation

1. Nest-building in birds is a(n) ____, or inherited behavior.
2. An action that aids survival is a(n) ____.
3. Responding to bright light by blinking is an example of ____.
4. A change that causes a reaction is a(n) ____.
5. A quick, automatic response to a stimulus is a(n) ____.
6. The process by which organisms best adapted to an environment survive is ____.
7. The sharp teeth of a tiger is an example of a(n) ____.
8. An inherited trait that helps a species survive in its environment is a(n) ____.
9. A reaction to a stimulus is a(n) ____.

10. Genetic changes in species over time is ___.

11. All the organisms of a species that live in a certain place is a(n) ___.

Explaining Science

Write a paragraph or create an outline to explain these questions.

1. Describe three adaptations that help organisms survive.

2. What evidence do scientists have to support evolution?

3. Give an example of how populations that become isolated might evolve.

4. How are sensory organs important to organisms?

5. List four ways you are responding to your environment right now. What is the stimulus and response in each example?

Using Skills

1. Suppose you discovered a fossil of a new species. The fossil is of an organism with two large webbed feet, two winglike structures, and two large ears. What **conclusions** can you **draw** about the organism?

2. **Predict** what might happen to the peppered moth population in the cities of England if pollution from smokestacks is reduced. Give reasons for your predictions.

3. **Observe** the frog on page A87. What adaptations can you identify? Tell how each might help the frog survive.

Critical Thinking

1. Think about ways you respond to stimuli that help you survive. **Classify** each behavior as an instinct, reflex, or learned behavior.

2. **Suppose** you have found a fossil. Describe your imaginary fossil and **infer** about past life based on what you know about a similar organism that is alive today.

3. **Apply** Darwin's theory of natural selection to explain why the ptarmigan on page A92 changes color.

A World in Her Hands!

Imagine having a tiny world of your own to observe! The world in this girl's hands has a balanced supply of everything it needs. What can you do to help create, protect, and keep the natural balance in your world?

Chapter 4
Ecosystems and Biomes

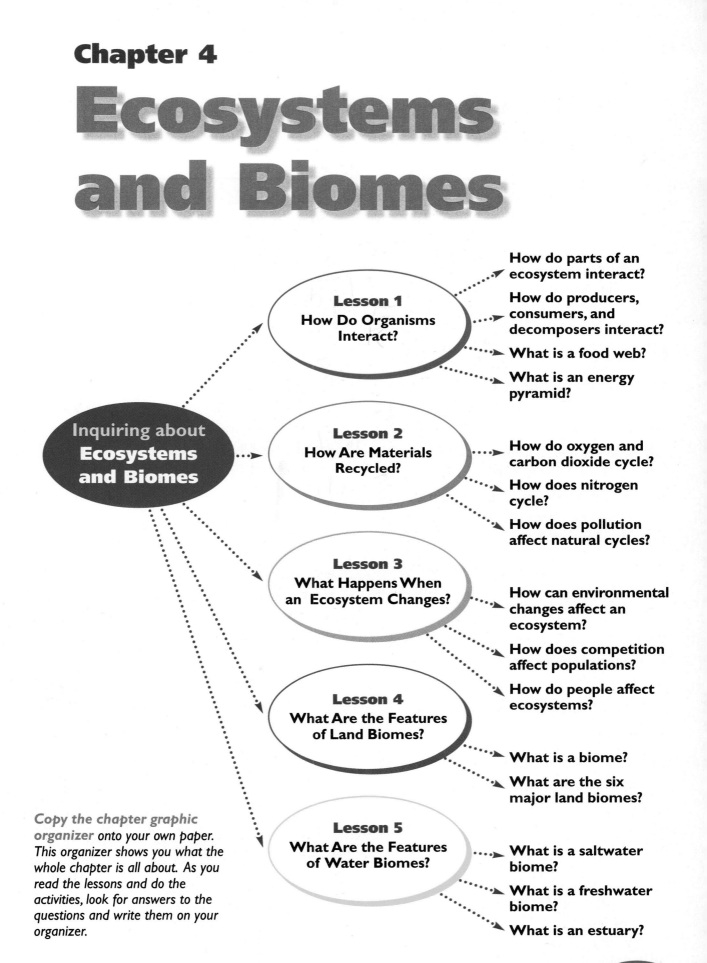

Inquiring about Ecosystems and Biomes

Lesson 1
How Do Organisms Interact?

- How do parts of an ecosystem interact?
- How do producers, consumers, and decomposers interact?
- What is a food web?
- What is an energy pyramid?

Lesson 2
How Are Materials Recycled?

- How do oxygen and carbon dioxide cycle?
- How does nitrogen cycle?
- How does pollution affect natural cycles?

Lesson 3
What Happens When an Ecosystem Changes?

- How can environmental changes affect an ecosystem?
- How does competition affect populations?
- How do people affect ecosystems?

Lesson 4
What Are the Features of Land Biomes?

- What is a biome?
- What are the six major land biomes?

Lesson 5
What Are the Features of Water Biomes?

- What is a saltwater biome?
- What is a freshwater biome?
- What is an estuary?

Copy the chapter graphic organizer onto your own paper. This organizer shows you what the whole chapter is all about. As you read the lessons and do the activities, look for answers to the questions and write them on your organizer.

Exploring a Water Ecosystem

Process Skills

- predicting
- observing
- inferring
- communicating

Materials

- masking tape
- plastic bottle with top portion removed
- metric ruler
- small pebbles
- aquarium water
- elodea plant
- marker

Explore

1 Use masking tape to cover the cut edge of a plastic bottle from which the top portion has been removed.

 Safety Note *Handle the cut bottle carefully. The edges may be sharp.*

2 Place about 1 cm of pebbles in the bottom of the plastic bottle. Add water to a depth of about 8 cm.

3 Add an elodea plant to your water ecosystem. Be sure the roots of the plant are anchored in the pebbles.

4 With a marker, mark the water level of your ecosystem on the side of the bottle.

5 **Predict** what will happen to the water level after several days. Record your prediction.

6 **Observe** your ecosystem for at least 3 days. Record your observations.

Reflect

What can you **infer** from your predictions and observations? **Communicate** your observations to your classmates. Make a list of possible explanations for what you observed.

? Inquire Further

What might happen if you placed a land ecosystem above the water ecosystem? How might this affect the water level in the water ecosystem? Develop a plan to answer these or other questions you may have.

Making Predictions

As you read Lesson 1, *How Do Organisms Interact?*, you'll be **making predictions**. A prediction is an educated guess about what may happen in the future. When making a prediction, rely on the information provided, as well as what you already know about similar events. Assume that what happened in the past could happen again.

Example

Look at the food chain to the right. To make a prediction about how this food chain would change if all the grass died, follow these steps:

1. Identify the events or actions provided in the picture.

2. Think about how the events and actions might be related.

3. Identify a similar situation. Recall what happened there.

4. Use the information from the picture and the past situation to make a prediction.

Talk About It!

1. What information can you gain from analyzing the food chain?

2. Predict what would happen to the number of owls if the number of crickets decreased.

Reading Vocabulary

prediction, an educated guess about what may happen in the future

You will learn:

- how parts of an ecosystem interact.
- how producers, consumers, and decomposers interact.
- what a food web is.
- what an energy pyramid is.

Like other ecosystems on Earth, this park has both living and nonliving parts. ▼

Lesson 1

How Do Organisms Interact?

Shhh! What could THAT be? It's the end of a long day on your camping trip. Your campfire is just glowing embers. You get the feeling you're being watched. You wonder what animal might be rustling around out there in the dark.

Interactions Within Ecosystems

You could spend hours looking through field guides before you figure out what might be lurking in a forest. A forest is full of different kinds of living things, including animals, plants, mushrooms, molds, algae, and microscopic one-celled organisms. All the living things in a forest interact with each other. They also interact with nonliving parts of the forest.

The city park shown on these pages is also made up of different living and nonliving things that interact. A park and a forest are both examples of ecosystems. Each ecosystem includes the living and nonliving parts that affect the organisms living there. An ecosystem can be small like a puddle or vast like the ocean.

People, dogs, grass, shrubs, trees, flowers, birds, squirrels, insects, spiders, and worms—these are some of the living things you might find in this park ecosystem. What are some of the nonliving things you might find in a park?

Air, water in a pond or puddle, soil, rocks, concrete sidewalks, and park benches are a few of the nonliving parts of a park ecosystem. What other living or nonliving parts can you think of?

To survive in a park ecosystem, organisms must be adapted to the environmental conditions of the park—the kind of soil, the temperature of the air, and the amount of light and water. In fact, the nonliving parts of an ecosystem often determine what organisms live there. For example, cactus plants don't normally live in a park like this one. Cactuses live in hotter, dryer ecosystems that have sandier soil than this park does.

Each organism in an ecosystem is also affected by the other organisms living there. Look at the grass growing on the ground in the park. The grass has a thick root system that is able to spread new grass tufts through the field. The grass roots hold moisture in the soil. When grass blades die and decay, they make the soil rich. The moisture and nutrients in the soil enable other plants to grow. Other plants you might see in the park include dandelions and clovers, as well as garden flowers.

Insects are attracted by the grasses and other plants in the park. If you look closely near ground level, you might see grasshoppers, crickets, honeybees, butterflies, or fireflies. Animals are attracted by the insects and plants. If you look underground, you might find burrowing animals, such as ground squirrels, earthworms, or garter snakes.

Now, think about what's above the ground. Birds, such as cardinals, fly through the air and land on the ground, looking for seeds. Other birds, such as robins, seek out worms for their meals. All these parts make up a healthy park ecosystem. A healthy ecosystem is one in which the living and nonliving parts are balanced.

Glossary

herbivore (hėr′bə vôr), a consumer that eats only plants or other producers

carnivore (kär′nə vôr), a consumer that eats only animals

omnivore (om′ni vôr), a consumer that eats both producers and consumers

Producers, Consumers, and Decomposers

When you read about life processes in Chapter 3, you learned that living things are alike in that they all must get the energy they need to carry on other life processes. However, organisms vary in how they get energy. How do you get energy?

Green plants are different from you and most other organisms. They get energy from food that they make during photosynthesis. During this process, a green plant uses sunlight to change carbon dioxide and water into glucose, a type of sugar. The sugar is stored by the plant until the plant needs energy. Then the plant releases the stored energy. Because green plants produce their own food, they are called producers.

Most other organisms can't use sunlight to make their own food as plants can. Instead, they get energy by eating, or consuming, food. These organisms are called consumers. What's the food that consumers eat? It's other organisms.

Some consumers, like the insects in the picture, feed directly on plants. They get the energy they need to carry on life processes from the stored energy in the plant leaves. Other consumers eat animals. A bird, for example, may come along and snatch one of the insects shown. It gets its energy from the energy in the insect.

One type of consumer, called an **herbivore,** eats only plants. Beavers are herbivores because they feed on the bark of aspen, birch, willow, and other trees. Caterpillars, deer, rabbits, ducks, and elephants are other examples of herbivores. Other consumers, called **carnivores**, eat only other animals. The brown bat is a carnivore because it feeds only on insects. Tigers, hawks, weasels, frogs, pelicans, and killer whales are other examples of carnivores.

Still other consumers, called **omnivores**, eat both plants and animals. A skunk is an omnivore because it eats plants, insects, and worms.

These caterpillars are consumers because they feed on plants. ▼

What are you—an herbivore, a carnivore, or an omnivore? You probably answered that humans are omnivores because they eat both plants and animals. In fact, humans eat plants, animals, fungi, and even certain bacteria.

Did you ever think about what happens to all the leaves that fall off trees in autumn? Do you know what happens to the body of an animal that dies in the forest? Eventually, the bodies of dead organisms disappear. Every ecosystem contains consumers called **decomposers**. These organisms get nutrients and energy from dead bodies and the wastes of living organisms. Decomposers break down the wastes and complex chemicals in dead organisms into simple chemicals. These simple chemicals can then be used again by plants.

Fungi, such as molds and mushrooms, are decomposers. You've probably seen molds growing on food, or perhaps you've noticed mushrooms like the one shown here growing on the ground or on trees. Some species of bacteria are also decomposers. Without decomposers, all ecosystems on the earth would soon be piled high with dead organisms and their wastes!

In general, plants are producers, and animals are consumers. However, one special producer is not a plant. In fact, this producer, a type of bacteria, does not even depend on sunlight to make its own food!

Sunlight can't reach the deep ocean floor, so no photosynthesis can occur. In these places, hot plumes of water rise from small vents on the ocean floor. Sulfur-containing compounds, called sulfides, are dissolved in the water. Unusual bacteria around the vents use oxygen and sulfides from the water to release energy. With this energy, they convert carbon dioxide and water into sugars. Therefore, in this ecosystem, bacteria are the producers. The tube worms, giant clams, and other organisms seen in the picture are consumers.

Sulfides from within the earth are the original energy source for organisms of the deep-ocean vent ecosystem. These tubeworms eat the bacteria that convert these sulfur-containing compounds to chemical energy. ▶

Glossary

decomposer
(dē′kəm pō′zər), an organism that obtains energy by consuming dead organisms and the wastes of living organisms

Glossary

▲ *Decomposers like this scarlet waxy cap mushroom break down dead organisms and return nutrients to the soil.*

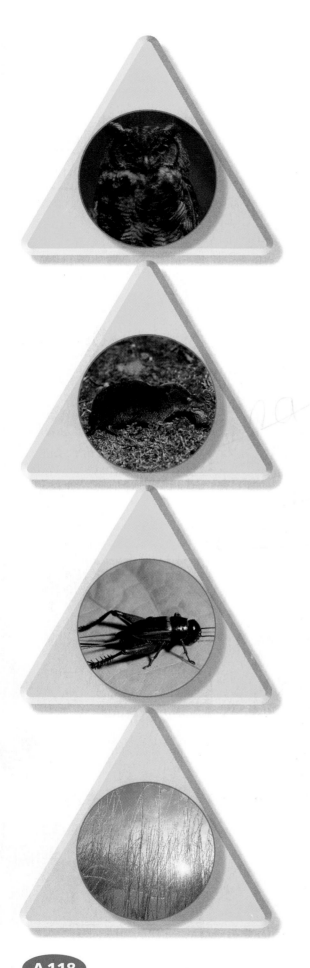

Food Webs

The pictures show some organisms you might find in a field. The grass plants in the bottom picture convert light energy from the sun, water, and carbon dioxide into sugar that has stored energy. The cricket eats the grass plant, transferring the plant's energy and nutrients to itself. Later, the cricket is eaten by a shrew. The shrew lives on energy and nutrients it gets from eating the cricket. Even later, the shrew is eaten by the owl. The owl lives on energy and nutrients from the shrew's body.

As you can see from this diagram, energy and nutrients move through organisms within an ecosystem. Arrows in the diagram show the direction in which energy and nutrients are transferred from one organism to the next. Producers, such as grass plants, are eaten by consumers. Those consumers are eaten by other consumers. A model such as this that shows how energy moves in an ecosystem is called a food chain. The grass, the cricket, the shrew, and the owl are all links in this food chain.

When the owl dies, decomposers will get energy by breaking down the owl's body. The minerals and gases that are released in this process become nutrients that can be used again by plants. Decomposers make up the final link in any food chain.

You probably know that crickets in a field are not the only animals that eat grass plants. A rabbit also eats grass. A snake might eat the rabbit, and an owl might eat the snake. In this food chain, the grass, the rabbit, the snake, and the owl are the links. Notice that the grass and the owl are links in both this food chain and the one shown to the left. Most organisms in an ecosystem are part of more than one food chain.

◀ *This is only one of the food chains you might find in a field ecosystem.*

Different food chains in an ecosystem are linked together in a food web. Study the food web below. In this food web, algae, water lilies, cattails, arrowheads, and duckweed are all producers. Notice the variety of consumers that eat these producers. Tadpoles, worms, and waterfleas eat the algae. Crayfish eat duckweed, but also eat worms. Perch and sunfish eat crayfish. In turn, the sunfish may be eaten by a bullfrog.

The arrows in this pond food web show the flow of energy and nutrients in each individual food chain. ▼

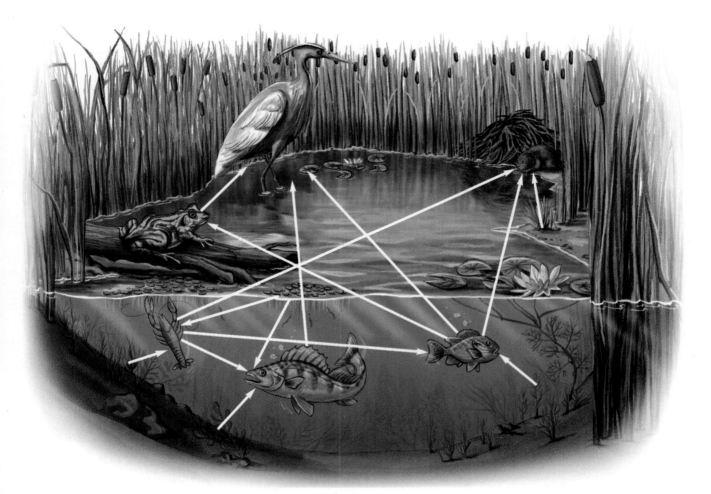

Notice, too, that all the organisms shown in this food web don't actually live in the water of the pond. Muskrats spend much of their time in the water, but also spend time on land. Look at the food web to find out what muskrats eat. A heron nests and sleeps on land. However, in early morning or evening, the heron flies to the pond to hunt for food. It stands quietly in shallow water, waiting to grab a fish or frog with its long, pointed beak. See how many food chains you can find that end with the heron.

Glossary

energy pyramid
(en′ər jē pir′ə mid), a model that shows how energy is used in a food chain or an ecosystem

Energy Pyramids

A food chain shows how energy moves from one organism to another. However, the same amount of energy does not move between organisms. Why not?

Remember that each organism needs energy for its life processes. Each organism uses some of the energy it gets from its food before it, in turn, becomes food for another organism. An **energy pyramid** is a model that can be used to show how energy is used in a particular food chain or ecosystem. The energy pyramid below shows the use and availability of energy in a grassy field.

The amount of energy available to a certain group of organisms depends on its feeding order in a food chain. In other words, it depends on which level of the pyramid it is on. Some energy is used at each link of a food chain to carry out life processes. That means less energy is available at any level in the pyramid than in the level below it. At which level is the least amount of energy available?

Most food chains have no more than five links. The reason is that the amount of energy left by the fifth link is only a small percentage of what was available at the first link.

Less and less energy is available as you near the top of an energy pyramid. ▼

The two energy pyramids below show how energy is transferred through organisms in the Arctic Ocean. The energy pyramid on the left shows a food chain with six links. The energy pyramid on the right shows a food chain with only three links. Notice that both food chains begin with algae and end with killer whales.

In the first food chain, energy is first transferred from algae to protists and zooplankton. Energy from these organisms is then transferred to squid. However, as the second pyramid shows, squid will also eat algae. When they do so, squid are at a lower level on the pyramid, and thus have more energy available to them. How does the amount of energy available to the killer whale differ in the two pyramids? If the killer whale feeds directly on squid, as shown in the second pyramid, much more energy is transferred to it. In any energy pyramid, the fewer the links in the food chain, the more energy that is available to the organisms at the top of the pyramid.

If the middle layers of consumers are eliminated, the same amount of producers can provide energy for more top consumers. ▼

Lesson 1 Review

1. How do parts of an ecosystem interact?
2. How do producers, consumers, and decomposers interact?
3. What are food webs?
4. What are energy pyramids?
5. **Predict**
   What might happen to the fish population in the food web shown on page A119 if the heron population disappeared?

Observing a Bottle Ecosystem

Process Skills

- predicting
- observing
- inferring

Materials

- gauze
- cup of water
- plastic bottle assembly
- water ecosystem from Explore Activity, page A112
- metric ruler
- pebbles
- graduated cup
- soil
- grass seed
- plastic wrap

Getting Ready

How do ecosystems interact? Do this activity to observe the interaction between a water ecosystem and a land ecosystem.

Use the water ecosystem that you made in the Explore Activity to complete this activity.

Follow This Procedure

❶ Make a chart like the one shown. Use your chart to record your observations.

Day	Observation
2	
4	
6	

❷ Place a piece of cotton gauze in a cup of water. Remove the gauze from the cup and squeeze out the excess water. Then thread the gauze through a hole in a plastic bottle cap. Screw the bottle cap onto the top part of the bottle.

❸ Assemble the bottle top and midsection as shown in Photo A.

❹ Place the assembly over the water ecosystem you made in the Explore Activity on page A112. Adjust the cotton gauze so that it is just above the bottom of your water ecosystem (Photo B).

Photo A

Photo B

Photo C

5 Make a land ecosystem by placing 2 cm of pebbles in the empty bottle top. Add about 240 mL of soil. Make sure the cotton gauze is in the soil—not stuck to the side of the bottle.

6 Sprinkle some grass seed evenly over the soil. Sprinkle water on the soil to make it moist but not soggy. Place plastic wrap over the top of the bottle (Photo C).

7 Think about how the two ecosystems will interact over several days. **Predict** what will happen to both the land and water ecosystem. Tell what information you used to make your prediction.

8 **Observe** your land and water ecosystems for several days. Record observations.

Interpret Your Results

1. Review your observations of the land and water ecosystems. What interactions did you observe between the two ecosystems?

2. Make an **inference.** What do you think would happen to the ecosystems if you added more plants?

Inquire Further

Would doubling the number of plants affect the ecosystem? Develop a plan to answer this or other questions you may have.

Self-Assessment

- I followed instructions to make a combination land and water ecosystem.
- I **predicted** what would happen to the land and water ecosystems over time.
- I tested my prediction.
- I recorded my **observations** about the ecosystems for several days.
- I made an **inference** about how the two ecosystems are related.

What's the Big Idea?

You will learn:

- how oxygen and carbon dioxide cycle.
- how nitrogen cycles.
- how pollution affects natural cycles.

Oxygen and carbon dioxide cycle through the living parts of an ecosystem. ▼

How Are Materials Recycled?

Hey! Look at that tiny leaf! Did you know that it not only traps the sun's energy to make food for other living organisms, but it also helps you breathe? Do you know how?

Oxygen-Carbon Dioxide Cycle

You've seen how energy available to organisms lessens as it flows through a food chain. As long as the sun shines, however, energy on Earth can be replenished. Yet organisms also require certain materials in order to survive. Like energy, these materials move through the food chain. Unlike energy, they are not less available as they do so. These materials are naturally recycled.

Water is one of the most important materials required by organisms. You are probably familiar with how water is recycled through precipitation and evaporation. Like water, carbon dioxide and oxygen are essential materials that also cycle within ecosystems. Recall that during photosynthesis green plants use energy from sunlight to combine carbon dioxide and water. Sugars and oxygen are produced. The first equation below shows this process.

Photosynthesis

carbon dioxide + water + energy → sugar + oxygen

Respiration

sugar + oxygen → carbon dioxide + water + energy

Now look at the bottom equation on the previous page. It shows the process of **respiration,** through which energy is released in cells. During respiration, sugar and oxygen combine, and carbon dioxide and water are produced. How do the equations for photosynthesis and respiration compare?

Much of the oxygen released by plants during photosynthesis is used by organisms during respiration. The carbon dioxide produced during respiration is exhaled by animals and may later be used by plants. This exchange is called the oxygen-carbon dioxide cycle. Follow the cycle in the diagram below.

Glossary

respiration
(res′pə rā′shən), energy-producing process in which a cell combines oxygen with sugars and gives off carbon dioxide and water

Carbon dioxide

Oxygen

Nitrogen Cycle

Nitrogen is another material that cycles through an ecosystem. Its pathway is called the nitrogen cycle.

All living things need nitrogen in order to make the proteins they need to survive. Almost 80 percent of the earth's air is nitrogen gas, so it might seem like getting enough nitrogen wouldn't be a problem. However, most organisms can't use nitrogen gas directly from the air. The nitrogen gas must first be changed into nitrogen compounds. This change happens in two ways in the environment.

The first way nitrogen is changed into nitrogen compounds is by special bacteria and other microscopic organisms that live in the soil. The bacteria, known as nitrogen-fixing bacteria, grow in nodules on the roots of certain plants, such as peas, soybeans, and clover. You can see the nodules on the clover roots on the next page. These bacteria can change nitrogen in the air into nitrogen compounds. The nitrogen compounds dissolve in water. Plants are then able to take them up when they take in water through their roots. Animals are able to get the nitrogen they need when they eat plants.

Do you see the lightning in the diagram? It shows the second way in which nitrogen gas can be changed. When lightning flashes through the air, nitrogen combines with the oxygen in the air to form nitrogen compounds. These compounds combine with rainwater to form nitrogen compounds that plants can use.

Without the nitrogen that these bacteria produce during decomposition, nitrogen could not cycle through the environment. ▶

Getting nitrogen into the ground is only half the cycle. To complete the cycle, nitrogen must be returned to the air. Once nitrogen compounds are made into proteins by plants, they pass through food webs. Bacteria in food webs decompose waste products or dead organisms. During decomposition, nitrogen compounds may be changed to nitrogen gas. The nitrogen gas returns to the air, completing the nitrogen cycle.

◀ *The nodules on the roots of clover plants contain bacteria that change nitrogen into nitrogen compounds the plants can use.*

Glossary

pollution (pə lü′shən), anything produced that harms the environment

Pollution Affects the Cycles

People are part of many different ecosystems. Unfortunately, they also often cause **pollution** that harms these ecosystems. Some pollution occurs naturally, such as when a volcano erupts and sends dust and poison gases into the air. However, most pollution is caused by people.

Some pollution disturbs the natural recycling of materials in the environment. For example, humans have disturbed the oxygen-carbon dioxide cycle by burning fossil fuels. Coal, oil, and natural gas are fossil fuels that are burned to run cars and factories, to heat buildings, and to make electricity. When these fossil fuels are burned, carbon dioxide is released into the air. Carbon dioxide prevents heat from escaping back into space from Earth.

Scientists have drilled into the core of glaciers and found evidence that carbon dioxide in the air has increased greatly since the 1700s. Some scientists think that this increase might be causing Earth's temperatures to rise. This effect is called global warming. Global warming may result in some of the polar ice melting. This melting might result in rising sea levels and flooding of low-lying coastal areas of land.

People have also disturbed the nitrogen cycle by using fertilizers that contain nitrogen compounds. In some places, fertilizer from farms seeps into the soil and

Through certain activities, humans pollute the air, water, soil, and groundwater. ▼

NO DUMPING

groundwater. Decomposers can't break down these nitrogen compounds fast enough, and they build up. Groundwater polluted by nitrogen compounds can be harmful to health, especially that of very young children.

To help control pollution, many laws have been passed by the U.S. government, as well as by states and local communities. Laws now require communities to treat sewage and to prevent factories from dumping chemicals.

Like the boy in the picture, you can do your part to reduce pollution by recycling newspapers, aluminum cans, glass bottles and jars, and plastics. You can also help by building a compost pile. Yard wastes, such as grass and leaves, and other plant matter, such as fruit and vegetable peels, can be mixed with soil. If the pile is kept moist, decomposers will recycle the materials, and you will have nutrient-rich soil to use on your garden or lawn.

Lesson 2 Review

1. Describe how oxygen and carbon dioxide cycle through the environment.

2. How does nitrogen cycle through the environment?

3. How does pollution affect the natural recycling of materials in an ecosystem?

4. **Predict**
   How might the oxygen–carbon dioxide cycle be affected if most of the trees in an ecosystem were destroyed?

When materials are recycled, they can be reused. That makes manufacturing new materials, which can cause pollution, less necessary. ▼

What's the Big Idea?

You will learn:

- how environmental changes can affect an ecosystem.
- how competition affects populations.
- how people affect ecosystems.

Lesson 3

What Happens When an Ecosystem Changes?

C-R-A-C-K! Lightning strikes a tree in the forest, setting it ablaze. A lack of rain has left the forest dry. The fire spreads rapidly from tree to tree and through the underbrush. How will such a fire change the forest ecosystem?

Environmental Changes

Changes are a natural part of the history of any ecosystem. Fires, droughts, floods, or shifts in temperature can and do change ecosystems.

As conditions in an ecosystem change, populations in the ecosystem might also change. All organisms have a certain range of conditions in which they can survive. Think about temperature, for example. As you see below, one species of fish may be able to tolerate only a narrow range of temperatures in cooler water. Another species, however, can tolerate a much wider range of temperatures. What do you think would happen if the water in which these fish lived became warmer?

This picture shows an example of how different species of fish can tolerate different ranges of temperature. ▼

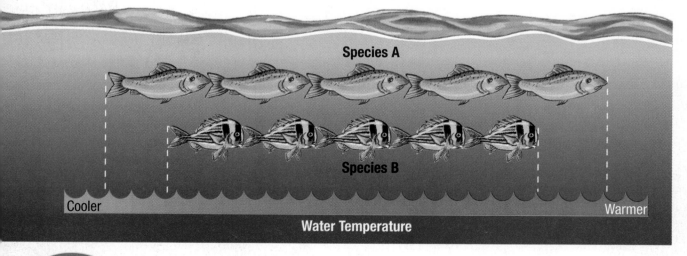

Species A

Species B

Cooler

Warmer

Water Temperature

The amount of light an ecosystem gets is also a condition that affects its populations. Coral polyps are small marine animals that build limestone shells. These shells build up to form colorful coral reefs, like the one shown below. Coral reefs can grow only in ocean waters that are warmer than 25°C and less than 10 meters deep. A change in world climates could cause a rise in sea levels. As a result, less light would reach the coral reefs. If the amount of light dipped under the range necessary for coral polyps to survive, the corals would die, and the entire ecosystem might be destroyed.

You have probably read or seen stories about an event called El Niño. Every few years, the westward-blowing trade winds in the Pacific Ocean reverse direction, and a mass of warm water flows eastward along the equator. El Niño causes environmental changes worldwide, from floods in California to droughts in Australia. Ecosystems change as a result. For example, off the coast of South America, higher water temperatures kill plankton and fish. Birds that feed on fish may starve, or they abandon their nests.

In any ecosystem, populations change as conditions change. New populations that can tolerate the new conditions move in. A new community of organisms is established, creating a new and different ecosystem.

▲ These soft corals are one of the many species you might find around a coral reef.

You can find a large variety of species around most coral reefs. ▼

Glossary

competition
(kom′pə tish′ən), a
situation in which two or
more organisms attempt
to use the same resource

Competition

Within an ecosystem, populations of different species live together and interact. You've already learned that one way organisms in an ecosystem interact is as consumers and producers in food webs.

Another way organisms in an ecosystem interact is by **competition**. Organisms can live only in ecosystems where their needs are met. These needs include food, water, space, shelter, light, minerals, and gases. These resources, however, are in limited supply in an ecosystem. When two or more organisms try to use the same resource, competition results. Members of different species may compete for food, water, and space. Members of the same species may also compete for these resources and for mates.

Think about the prairie ecosystem shown below. Populations of grasses, grasshoppers, mice, bison, and hawks all live together in the prairie ecosystem. Grasshoppers, mice, and bison compete for food because all three species eat plants. All organisms in the prairie ecosystem compete for water.

The mice that live in the prairie ecosystem compete with each other too—for space, food, water, and mates. As the population of mice becomes larger, competition among the mice increases. Not all the mice will survive. Competition is one way that the size of a population is controlled naturally.

Suppose that one year the prairie did not receive as much rain as usual. The lack of rain would limit the growth of the grasses and thistles. The reduced amount of these plants, in turn, would affect the populations of other

Organisms within an ecosystem compete for resources. How do the plants in the prairie compete? ▼

organisms. Less grass to eat would increase competition among grass-eaters. Fewer mice and grasshoppers would survive. In turn, the hawks that feed on the mice, like the one to the right, would be affected. Competition for food would also increase among hawks. How might this increase in competition affect the hawk population?

Whenever resources are limited, the organisms that survive will be those that are best adapted to the new conditions. These organisms are the ones that can best compete. For example, the grasslands of the African savannah have only two seasons, rainy and dry. When the dry season arrives, grass blades on the savannah turn brown, curl, and die. Acacia trees shed their leaves. However, both the acacias and the underground parts of the grasses live off stored food until the rains return. Both species are adapted to survive the dry conditions. In the meantime, most of the plant-eating animals, such as zebras and wildebeests, leave and move to new feeding grounds. Some of the weaker members of these migrating herds— especially the very young and the very old—may not survive the move.

What happens to the organisms of the savannah that don't migrate? Frogs, toads, and hedgehogs bury themselves in the ground, where they sleep until the rains return. As waterholes dry up, elephants often use their tusks to dig into the ground in search of water. As the grasses die off, elephants peel bark from trees to get moisture and food. When they can no longer find enough water and food, they move to areas where they can.

Lions change their diets during the dry season. With no zebras or wildebeests to eat, they compete to feed on warthogs and other small animals. Some lions may die during the dry season, but those that are the best hunters will probably survive.

▲ Hawks soar and circle over the prairie for long periods of time, competing to find mice or other small mammals for their next meal.

▲ *How have people changed this ecosystem? What effect will this have on the ecosystem?*

Purple loosestrife is only one of many introduced plants that have damaged ecosystems. ▶

People Affect Ecosystems

Ecosystems change naturally, but they may also be changed by humans. All the materials that people use and the food that people eat come from the environment. As people use these resources, such as the trees to the left, they change the ecosystems from which the resources come.

People have cut or burned forests, drained wetlands, and dammed or altered the courses of rivers. They have made these changes to make room for farms, roads, and houses, or to provide water, electricity, and other materials. As forests and wetlands disappear, animals and other organisms lose their homes and territories. They are less able to find food. Some populations of organisms—even entire species—may disappear forever.

People also change ecosystems when they introduce new species to areas. For example, the purple loosestrife pictured below did not naturally grow in the United States. It was introduced from Europe. With no natural predators or diseases, the plant crowded out other wetland plants. It spread rapidly and uncontrollably.

Ten thousand years ago, when people first developed farming, there were about 10 million people on Earth. By 1997, there were almost 6 billion people—about 600 times more. More than a quarter of a million people are added to the world's population every day. As the human population grows, its effect on the environment increases.

Mining coal, oil, and natural gas from the earth damages or causes risks to many ecosystems. However, people all over the world are taking steps to protect the environment. Through conservation methods, less fuel is needed. More energy-efficient cars, such as this electric car, also help. Recycling paper saves forest ecosystems, and using less water helps preserve wetland, river, and lake ecosystems. How are the people below acting to protect the environment?

▲ Electric cars help protect the environment because they don't use fossil fuels, which can harm the environment.

◀ Many groups work to restore ecosystems that have been damaged by people. These people are restoring a prairie by replanting natural species.

Lesson 3 Review

1. How can environmental changes affect an ecosystem?

2. How does competition affect populations?

3. Describe two ways that people affect ecosystems.

4. **Predict**
   What might happen to the ecosystem shown in the picture at the bottom of these pages if an insect that ate purple loosestrife were introduced into the environment?

What's the Big Idea?

You will learn:

- what a biome is.
- what the six major land biomes are.

Glossary

biome (bī′ōm), large geographic region with a particular kind of climate and community

▲ The climates in these two biomes are very different. As a result, the kinds of organisms in each are also different.

Lesson 4

What Are the Features of Land Biomes?

The sun is HOT—beating down on you. The air is so dry that your throat is parched. The few plants you can see are covered with spines. Not many animals seem to be around. Do you know where you are?

Biomes

If the place that you are standing is hot and very dry with few plants and animals, you could probably guess that you are in a desert. The hot, dry air is your first clue. The spiny plants and lack of animals is your second.

On land, a number of major types of ecosystems are described by their climates and the communities of organisms that live there. Similar ecosystems with similar climates and communities are called **biomes**. These large geographic regions are found in many locations around the earth. For example, desert biomes are found on almost every continent.

Climate is one of the most important factors that determines the kinds of organisms found in a biome. For example, some plants need more water than other plants. Plants such as large broadleaf trees can't live in biomes that receive little yearly precipitation, as cactus plants can. Some animals require cooler yearly temperatures than others do. Do you think a polar bear could survive in a desert? Why?

The kinds of plants that live in a biome determine the kinds of animals that live there. For example, grasslands support large populations of grass-eating animals, such as gazelles, as well as large predators that feed on them, such as lions. You won't find either in a desert biome, where little grass can grow.

Biomes change as latitude—or distance from the equator—changes because climate changes with latitude. At latitudes near the equator, the sun appears at the highest angle in the sky. Therefore, regions near the equator have the warmest climates. At latitudes near the poles, the sun is never very high in the sky. These places have the coldest climates. In the middle latitudes, the sun is rather high in the sky in summer and rather low in winter. These places have climates with seasonal changes.

Climate is also affected by altitude. As you hike up a mountain or travel closer to the poles, temperatures drop and climates change. Notice in the diagram how biomes change on a mountain.

The map on the next two pages shows the locations of the six major land biomes of the earth. Refer to this map as you read the rest of the chapter.

If you travel up a mountain in North America, you see biomes change in the same way as they do if you travel northward toward the North Pole. ▼

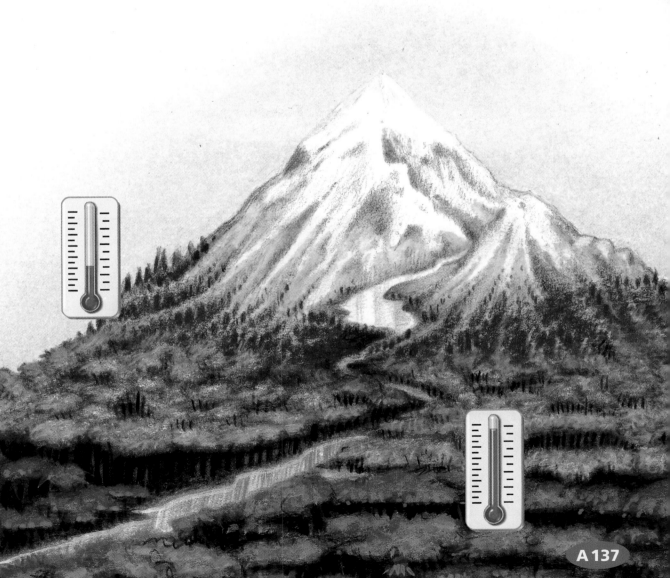

World Biomes

The type of climate of each biome is indicated by the yearly temperatures and precipitation. Look at the map and find the biome in which you live. What other biomes have you traveled to?

Tundra	Taiga	Temperate Deciduous Forest
Yearly temperatures: −57°C to 10°C Average precipitation: 20 cm	Yearly temperatures: −29°C to 22°C Average precipitation: 50 cm	Yearly temperatures: −20°C to 35°C Average precipitation: 125 cm

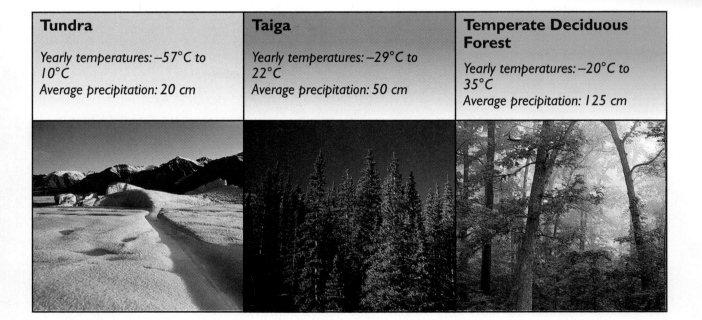

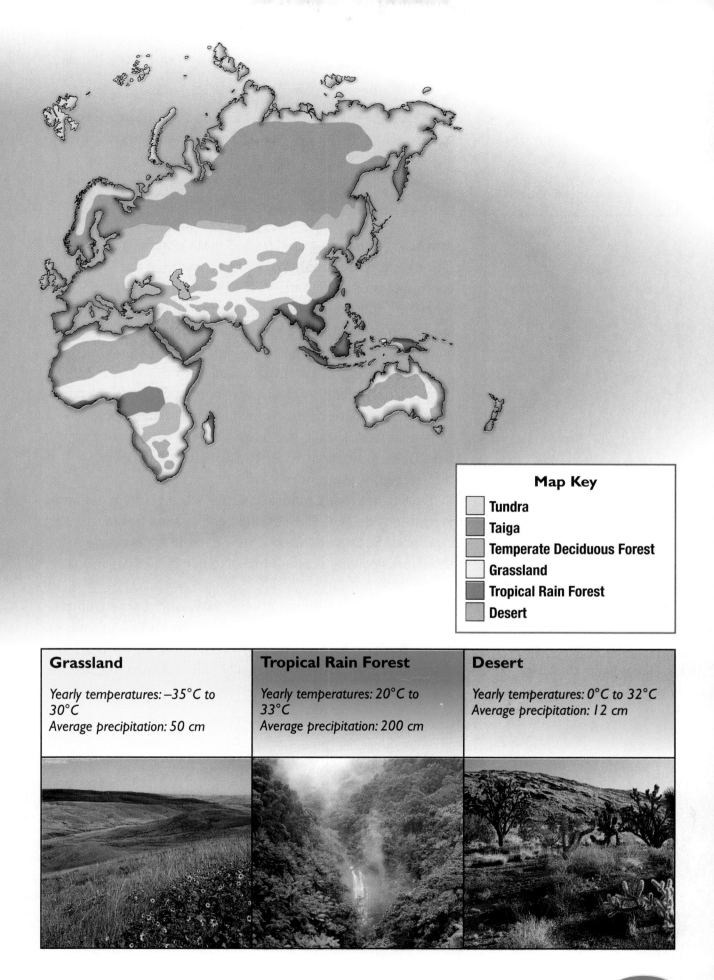

Map Key

- Tundra
- Taiga
- Temperate Deciduous Forest
- Grassland
- Tropical Rain Forest
- Desert

Grassland

Yearly temperatures: −35°C to 30°C
Average precipitation: 50 cm

Tropical Rain Forest

Yearly temperatures: 20°C to 33°C
Average precipitation: 200 cm

Desert

Yearly temperatures: 0°C to 32°C
Average precipitation: 12 cm

Glossary

tundra (tun′drə), the northernmost and coldest biome

permafrost (pėr′mə frôst′), ground that is permanently frozen

Land Biomes

Tundra

Can you imagine living in a biome that has very cold, harsh weather about nine months of the year and completely frozen ground during that time? These are the conditions in the **tundra** biome—the coldest and most northern biome. During the three months of warmer weather, the top few centimeters of ground thaw. The ground below, called **permafrost,** remains frozen. Ice that melts in the top layers can't seep into the ground, so it forms lakes, ponds, and marshy areas.

In most areas of tundra, the soil is so thin that it can support only plants with shallow roots. The soil lacks nutrients because decay happens very slowly in cold temperatures. In fact, the frozen bodies of animals that have been extinct for thousands of years have been discovered in the tundra.

During the short tundra summer, small plants grow and form seeds quickly. Mosses and lichens, seen below, are also common. Because all food chains depend on producers, the short growing season limits the number of organisms in this biome.

Animals do live on the tundra, however. Some animals you might find include polar bears, wolves, caribou, and mice. Birds include geese, ptarmigans, and snowy owls like the one below. Insects, especially flies and mosquitoes, are plentiful during the short summer.

The snowy owl feeds on small mammals, especially lemmings, and ptarmigan in the tundra. ▼

Taiga

Just south of the tundra in the Northern Hemisphere is the **taiga**, or coniferous forest biome. In the United States, you can find taiga in parts of Alaska, Maine, and Michigan and in the mountains of western states. Have you ever visited Yellowstone National Park in Wyoming or Yosemite and Sequoia National Parks in California? If so, you've visited the taiga. Look back at the map. Where else in the world can you find the taiga biome?

The taiga has cold winters, but its summers are longer and warmer than those of the tundra. Longer, warmer summers allow the ground to thaw completely, so there is no permafrost.

The most common plants in the taiga are conifers—trees such as pines, firs, spruces, cedars, and redwoods. Conifer trees, like those you see to the right, bear seeds in cones and do not lose all their leaves at one time. The plentiful trees of the taiga provide food and shelter for animals. However, they also shade the forest floor, so many low-lying shrubs and flowering plants can't grow. The needles and branches that fall to the forest floor take a long time to decay. Can you guess why? Most decomposers in the taiga are fungi.

Common mammals of the taiga include black bears, elk, moose, wolves, porcupines, mice, and squirrels. Birds include hawks, owls, geese, gray jays, and black-capped chickadees.

Glossary

taiga (tī′gə), forest biome just south of the tundra, characterized by conifers

The needles on these trees in this conifer forest are adapted to help the plants survive the cold, windy conditions of the taiga. ▼

Glossary

temperate deciduous forest

(tem′pər it di sij′ü es fôr′ist), forest biome characterized by trees that lose their leaves each year

Temperate Deciduous Forest

▲ The leaves of deciduous trees such as oaks change color in autumn, before they fall from the trees. New green leaves bud in the spring.

If you live in or near woods in the eastern United States, you probably live in the **temperate deciduous forest** biome. This biome gets its name from the trees that grow there. Trees that shed their leaves each autumn are deciduous trees. Maples, beeches, willows, and oaks, whose leaves you see here, are examples.

The annual fall of leaves in the forest provides food for worms, fungi, and bacteria. These organisms break down the leaves and recycle the nutrients from the leaves into the forest soil. Under the rich top layer of soil is usually a deeper layer of clay.

The temperate deciduous forest has four seasons. You probably know what they are. Winters are cold, summers are hot, and spring and autumn are mild.

Because of the rich soil, relatively short winters, and much precipitation, many kinds of plants grow in the deciduous forest. In addition to trees, you'll find shrubs, mosses, and small flowering plants. The plant life supports a variety of animal life, including eagles and owls, deer, chipmunks, raccoons, quail, snakes, and salamanders. The animals live in different layers of the forest—in the trees, in the shrubs, on and under the ground.

The picture shows forestland being cleared. When European settlers arrived in North America, they cut down large areas of the forests for farming. Much of the forest today is second-growth forest.

◄ Settlers cut trees to make room for growing crops. The temperate deciduous forest is not as extensive as it once was.

Grassland

Did you eat any of the foods in the picture today? These foods come from another biome—the **grassland**. In grasslands, the temperatures and seasons are similar to those in temperate deciduous forests. However, the precipitation is less, and dry periods occur often. That difference is important. It results in a different major form of plant life. Because grasslands get less rain, few trees grow there. As you can guess, grasses do. Grasses can survive the dry periods because they have root systems that spread out over large areas. When rains come, new plants sprout from the roots.

On the world biome map, you'll notice that grasslands are found in many places. Different species of grasses grow in different grasslands.

The soil of grasslands is very fertile. Each winter, the tops of many grasses die off. Decomposers act on the dead grass and return nutrients to the soil. Bacteria, fungi, worms, and burrowing animals live on or in the soil. On the grasslands of North America, bison, pronghorns, rabbits, prairie dogs, and mice feed. Coyotes, bobcats, badgers, and snakes eat the grass-eaters. Grassland birds include meadowlarks, plovers, and prairie chickens.

Grasslands have been called the "breadbaskets" of the world because, as you can see below, they are ideal for growing grass cereal grains. Wheat, corn, rice, oats, rye, barley, sorghum, millet, and sugarcane are all grasses used in food products. Grasses also provide most of the food for farm animals, such as cattle and sheep.

Glossary

grassland (gras′land), biome characterized by few trees and many grasses

▲ Grass seeds, or grains, provide food for people and animals around the world.

The wheat this tractor is harvesting is just one of the many food products that are grown in grasslands. ▼

Glossary

Glossary

tropical rain forest
(trop′ə kəl rān fôr′ist), biome that has much rainfall and high temperatures all year

Picture a biome where trees grow tall—50 meters or more. Beneath the tall trees are shorter trees that can grow in shade. In most areas, the trees form such a thick canopy that little sunlight reaches the forest floor. Only a few plants, such as ferns and mosses, grow there. However, vines hang from the trees, and orchids and other plants live on the branches of the trees.

Most animals in this biome live in the trees too. Parrots, monkeys, sloths, snakes, frogs, and butterflies all have adaptations for living in trees. Overripe fruits and dead leaves drop from trees, providing food for some organisms that live on the ground. Insects, molds, and bacteria quickly consume this food.

Can you guess which biome you're in? You're right—the **tropical rain forest**. This biome is located near the equator. Because of this location, the tropical rain forest has no seasons. Rainfall is heavy and temperatures are high all year round. More species of organisms live in the tropical rain forest than in all the other land biomes combined.

In the warm, moist conditions of the tropical rain forest, nutrients that are released into the soil are quickly taken up by the plants. As a result, the soil is thin and not very rich. The trees of the rain forest are the main storage place of nutrients. If the trees are removed, the entire ecosystem is disturbed. Yet much of the rain forest is being cleared for farmland. Crops use up soil nutrients quickly, and the sun bakes the soil into a hard claylike material.

Rain forests are important because many of the things you use come from them. Fruits, nuts, and spices come from the rain forest. Other rain forest plants are used to make medicines, perfumes and cosmetics, and latex for rubber.

The cacao tree grows in tropical rain forests. Its seeds are used to make chocolate. Some cacao tree farmers now plant their trees beneath the canopy of the rain forest instead of cutting it down. ▼

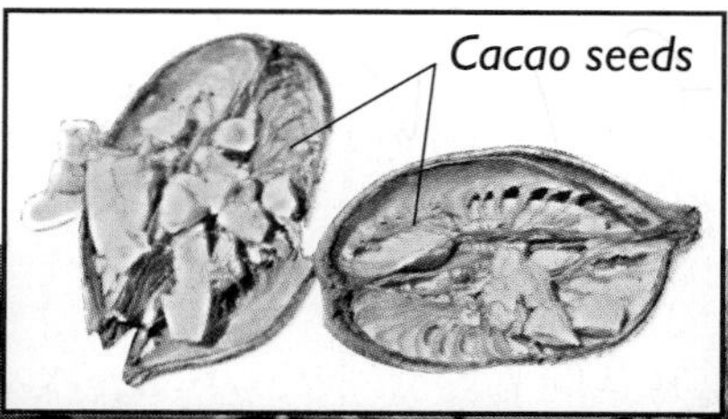

Desert

You may think of **deserts** as dry, hot places. It's true—all deserts are dry. The desert biome gets less than 25 centimeters of rain each year. The Atacama Desert in Chile is the driest place in the world, with an average annual rainfall of zero. Also, most deserts do have high temperatures during the day. But did you know that they can be cold at night? Temperatures might even drop to freezing. Some deserts, such as the Gobi Desert in Asia and the Patagonian Desert in South America, are cold for several months of the year.

Most people think of deserts as being covered with sand. Some deserts, like the Namib Desert in the top right photo, are sandy, but others, like the Creosote Bush Desert shown in the bottom photo, are covered in gravel and boulders.

Desert soils are usually low in nutrients. The dry conditions don't provide good environments for the decomposers that return nutrients to soil through decay.

Organisms that live in the desert have special adaptations that allow them to survive dry climate, poor soil, and wide temperature changes. Many animals spend the hottest part of the day underground. Some don't need to drink water very often because they can store a lot of water in their tissues. Cactus and other desert plants store water in their stems. What other adaptations make cactuses suited for the hot, dry environment they live in?

In some areas, grasslands that once bordered deserts have become part of the desert through overgrazing and drought. People are trying to restore these areas by replanting trees and other plants.

Glossary

desert (dez′ərt), biome with little rainfall and usually high daytime temperatures

▲ The Namib Desert in Namibia (top), is sandy, unlike the rocky desert in the Creosote Bush Desert in Death Valley, California (below).

Lesson 4 Review

1. What is a biome?

2. What are the six major land biomes?

3. **Predict**
   What do you think might happen to an orchid plant from the taiga if you moved it to a grassland? Explain.

Investigating Soils

Process Skills

Process Skills

- observing
- classifying
- communicating
- making operational definitions

Materials

- soil sample
- plastic cup
- distilled water
- spoon
- litmus paper
- clock with second hand

Getting Ready

The characteristics of the soil in a biome determine the kind of plants that will grow there. In this activity, you'll test your local soil for one important characteristic—acidity.

Follow This Procedure

1 Make a chart like the one shown. Use your chart to record your observations.

	Color of litmus paper
10 sec	
5 min	
15 min	

2 Collect a soil sample from your home or school yard in a plastic cup.

3 Slowly add distilled water to the soil as you stir it with a spoon. Keep adding water until the soil is muddy and about as thick as applesauce.

4 You will be using litmus paper to test how acidic the soil sample is. The litmus paper will change from blue to red if the soil is acidic.

5 Insert 3 strips of litmus paper halfway into the muddy soil (Photo A). Wait 10 seconds.

Photo A

Photo B

6 Remove one piece of litmus paper (Photo B). Dip it into a cup of distilled water to rinse off the soil. **Observe** the color of the litmus paper. Record this color in your chart.

7 If the litmus paper is blue, wait another 5 minutes. Then remove another piece of litmus paper from the soil. Repeat step 6.

8 If the second piece of litmus is blue, wait another 10 minutes and repeat step 6.

Interpret Your Results

1. Blue litmus paper turns red or pink in acid. Based on your observations, how would you **classify** your soil—acidic or not acidic?

2. Why do you think some acidic soils take longer than others to turn the litmus paper red? **Communicate** your ideas to your group.

3. An **operational definition** describes what an object does or what you can observe about it. Write an operational definition for an acidic soil.

? Inquire Further

How do you think changing the acidity of soil would affect the plants that grow there? Develop a plan to answer this or other questions you may have.

Self-Assessment

- I followed instructions to test the acidity of a soil sample.
- I made and recorded **observations** of the color of the litmus paper.
- I **classified** the soil sample as an acid or a non-acid.
- I **communicated** activity results to my group.
- I wrote an **operational definition** of an acidic soil.

What's the Big Idea?

You will learn:

- what a saltwater biome is.
- what a freshwater biome is.
- what an estuary is.

Glossary

saltwater biome (sȯlt′wȯ′tər bī′ōm), water biome that has a high salt content

plankton (plangk′tən), microscopic, free-floating organisms that serve as food for larger organisms

▲ Almost three-fourths of the earth's surface is covered by the saltwater biome.

Lesson 5

What Are the Features of Water Biomes?

You're at the beach, running into the water. The waves are splashing up your legs. Suddenly, a huge wave comes crashing in. You yell as it drenches you. **Yuk!** The water tastes awful. It's salty. You must be at the ocean!

Saltwater Biomes

About three-quarters of Earth's surface is covered by water. Like the land that covers Earth, the water areas, too, have biomes characterized by certain conditions and communities of organisms. A water biome that has a high salt content is called a **saltwater biome**. As you can see from the picture on the left, this biome is Earth's largest.

This saltwater biome can be divided into three different regions. The three zones differ in their physical characteristics and in the organisms that live there. As you read about each zone, find it in the picture on the next page.

The shallow ocean zone makes up only a small part of the saltwater biome. If you've ever been to the ocean, it's this zone that you're probably most familiar with. It occurs along the coasts of continents and islands. The water in this area is shallow enough for sunlight to reach the bottom. Water temperature changes little from day to night or from season to season.

The area of ocean away from the coast is divided into two zones—the ocean surface zone and the deep ocean zone. Sunlight can reach the top areas of the surface zone, but no light reaches the deep ocean. Also, as you go farther down into the ocean water, the temperature gets colder. How will the differences in temperature and light in these two zones affect the organisms that live there?

Shallow Ocean Zone

Food chains in this area depend mostly on *plankton*—free-floating organisms near the surface of the water. Clams, crabs, and worms live in the sand or mud on the bottom of this zone. Crabs, octopuses, and fish hide in crannies among the rocks. Jellyfish, turtles, corals, and sponges are some other organisms that live in this zone.

Ocean Surface Zone

Plankton live in the brightly lit top layers of the open ocean. They are the producers in the surface food chains. Because conditions in this zone are so favorable, more species live here than in any other zone. Animals that you might find here include tuna, sharks, jellyfish, rays, whales, and ocean birds, such as albatross.

Deep Ocean Zone

Not enough light reaches below 100 meters of the deep ocean water for photosynthesis to take place. As a result, less food is available and fewer species live here. Some organisms eat other deep water organisms. Others feed on the remains of dead organisms that sink from above. It is in this zone that you would find the ocean vents you read about in Chapter 3. Some of the creatures that live in the darkness of this zone have light-producing body parts that they use to attract mates or prey.

Glossary

freshwater biome
(fresh′wô′tər bī′ōm),
water biome that has a
low salt content

Freshwater Biomes

Most bodies of water other than the ocean, such as lakes, ponds, rivers, and streams, contain very little salt. Each of these bodies is a **freshwater biome** . Freshwater biomes can be divided into two types. Those that have standing water include lakes and ponds. Those that have running water include rivers and streams.

Lakes, like the one shown on this page, are larger and usually deeper than ponds. Most lakes are deep enough to have a colder, lower layer of water that receives little or no sunlight. Temperature and available sunlight determine the kinds of organisms that live in each area of a lake.

When you consider what you know about producers and food chains, you can probably guess that most organisms live near the upper, sunnier part of a lake. Floating duckweed plants and plants that grow in shallow water around the lake's edges form the basis of food chains. These food chains include fish, insects, frogs, turtles, beavers, and a variety of birds, including herons and grebes.

Few animals live in the deep part of a lake. Those that do live there include bacteria, worms, and other decomposers. They feed on the remains of dead organisms that settle to the lake bottom.

Mountain lakes like this one were formed when melting valley glaciers dumped a ridge of sand, gravel, and rocks across a river. Other lakes form in a variety of ways. ▼

The main difference between lakes and rivers or streams is the movement of water. Like the one shown here, the water in streams moves quickly. As a result, air is mixed with the water. This mixing adds oxygen to the water, which allows certain organisms, such as trout, frogs, and many insects, to live there. Do you notice anything about the shape of the fish that live in rapidly moving water? Can you guess how this shape allows them to travel in the river?

Mountain streams are made up of a series of fast, shallow, rocky stretches, called rapids, followed by pools of deeper, quieter water. While flowing through the rapids, the water picks up particles of sand, silt, and even gravel and carries them downstream. The result is that these areas are left as bare rock. Here insect larvae, algae, and some worms attach themselves to the rocky beds. In some areas, black fly larvae form such dense groups that they look like a carpet of black moss on the rocks.

As water flows through the rapids, it also sweeps food downstream to the quieter pools. There, water plants can root and not be washed away. Animals find plenty of food here. The pools also provide breeding areas for frogs.

Because stream water is constantly moving and mixing, a small stream will have a more constant temperature than would a pond. Daphnia and many other microscopic organisms are part of the food chain in this stream. ▼

Glossary

Glossary

estuary (es′chü er′ē), place where fresh water from rivers or streams mixes with saltwater from the ocean

Estuaries

Many rivers and streams empty into the ocean. Where fresh water from a river or stream mixes with saltwater from the ocean, an **estuary** forms.

Pieces of rock, soil, and other materials are washed into an estuary by both the river and the ocean tides. There they settle to form a muddy or sandy floor. Water in an estuary is usually warmer than ocean water and contains less salt. However, the salt content of the water changes with the tides. With high tide, more salty ocean water flows in. At low tide, when ocean water moves out, the water of the estuary becomes less salty.

Salt content is not the only thing that changes daily in an estuary. For part of the day, the entire area is under water. However, when the tide goes out, some of the sand or mud flats may be exposed to the sun. The remains of algae and other organisms begin to decay, returning nutrients to the estuary floor. There, plants such as cordgrasses, sea lavender, and spike grass provide food and shelter for many organisms.

Species that live in the estuary have adapted to the changing rhythm of the tides. For example, the air-breathing coffee bean snail climbs the stems of cordgrass twice a day as the tides come in. Nonflying insects also climb up plants to avoid high water. These insects provide insect-eating birds, such as marsh wrens and seaside sparrows, with an easy meal during high tide.

Many microscopic organisms like this Hyperia *provide food for estuary species.* ▼

An estuary is constantly changing, and the organisms that populate it must be adapted to living with daily changes in water level and salt content. ▼

Estuaries are important as breeding grounds for many birds and ocean organisms. Many fish lay their eggs in estuaries. When they hatch, young fish feed on the plentiful plankton. More than three-fourths of all the shellfish and seafood harvested in the United States spend their early lives in estuaries, including the crab shown here. These crabs, shrimp, and mussels provide food for diamondback terrapins and wading birds, such as the snowy egret and clapper rail.

Many migrating birds stop to rest and feed in estuaries. Snow geese, Canada geese, dabbling ducks, black ducks, and blue-winged teals all feed on estuary plants. Northern harriers and short-eared owls feed on mice and other small mammals in the estuary.

Have you ever eaten the meat from a crab? Chances are that crab began its life in an estuary. ▼

Lesson 5 Review

1. What is a saltwater biome?

2. What is a freshwater biome?

3. What is an estuary?

4. **Predict**
   Suppose a manufacturing company dumped harmful wastes into the river that empties into the estuary below. What changes might you see in the estuary over time?

Chapter 4 Review

Chapter Main Ideas

Lesson 1
• Living and nonliving parts of an ecosystem enable organisms to survive.
• The energy needed for life processes is trapped by producers and used by consumers and decomposers.
• Different food chains in an ecosystem are linked together in a food web.
• An energy pyramid is a model that shows how much energy is available at each level of a food chain or ecosystem.

Lesson 2
• Green plants use carbon dioxide and give off oxygen during photosynthesis. Plants and other organisms use oxygen and release carbon dioxide during respiration.
• Nitrogen cycles through an ecosystem in the nitrogen cycle.
• Pollution disturbs the natural recycling of materials in an ecosystem.

Lesson 3
• Environmental changes can change the populations in an ecosystem.
• Species often adapt or die off when populations compete for resources.
• People can change ecosystems by using resources or introducing new species.

Lesson 4
• Biomes are large geographic regions with a particular climate and community.
• The six major land biomes are the tundra, taiga, deciduous forest, tropical rain forest, grassland, and the desert.

Lesson 5
• A saltwater biome is a water biome that has a high salt content.
• A freshwater biome is a body of water such as a lake, pond, river, or stream that does not have a high salt content.
• An estuary is a water biome where fresh water mixes with salt water.

Reviewing Science Words and Concepts

Write the letter of the word or phrase that best completes each sentence.

a. biome
b. carnivore
c. competition
d. energy pyramid
e. estuary
f. herbivore
g. omnivore
h. permafrost
i. plankton
j. respiration
k. taiga
l. tundra

1. Ground that is always frozen is ___.
2. A region with a particular climate and community is called a(n) ___.
3. The process that releases energy in cells is known as ___.
4. A name for an animal-eating consumer is a(n) ___.
5. A coniferous forest biome is called a(n) ___.
6. A place where saltwater and fresh water mix is called a(n) ___.
7. A consumer that eats plants and animals is called a(n) ___.

8. The coldest and most northern biome is a region called the ___.

9. A microscopic food source found floating in oceans is called ___.

10. Organisms interact as they try to use the same resources when ___ occurs.

11. A plant-eating consumer is called a(n) ___.

12. A model of energy use in a food chain is represented as a(n) ___.

Explaining Science

Write a paragraph or create a dialogue for a radio show that explains these questions.

1. Why is the amount of available energy different for each type of organism in a food chain?

2. Give two examples of what can happen if natural cycles are disrupted by people.

3. How are populations affected by environmental changes?

4. How do climate, altitude, and latitude affect biomes?

5. What determines the amount and kinds of organisms that live in each area or zone of a water biome?

Using Skills

1. **Predict** what will happen next if you remove all the crickets from a field ecosystem.

2. Choose an ecosystem such as your schoolyard or a park. Make a list of six interactions that you **observe** in the ecosystem.

3. Identify three foods you ate today. Make a **model** of a food chain showing the path of energy in the food you ate.

Critical Thinking

1. Create a poster that will **compare** and **contrast** the six major land biomes.

2. Suppose you have a fish tank with several fish. A friend wants to give you two new fish for your tank. What information should you **evaluate** before you **make a decision** about whether or not to add the new fish?

3. Make a **model** of a water biome using a shoe box. Draw a scene and place three-dimensional items inside the box to represent organisms. Then cover the opening with plastic wrap instead of a lid.

Unit A Review

Reviewing Words and Concepts

Choose at least three words from the **Chapter 1** list below. Use the words to write a paragraph about how these concepts are related. Do the same for each of the other chapters.

Chapter 1
cell theory
chromosome
cytoplasm
mitochondria
organelles
species

Chapter 2
DNA
genes
inherit
meiosis
sex cells
sexual
   reproduction

Chapter 3
adaptation
evolution
inherited
  behavior
instinct
natural selection
reflex

Chapter 4
biome
competition
energy pyramid
grassland
pollution
taiga

Reviewing Main Ideas

Each of the statements below is false. Change the underlined word or words to make each statement true.

1. The <u>vacuole</u> is an organelle that puts together proteins for the cell.

2. Chloroplasts in plant cells contain <u>chromosomes</u> which use sunlight to make sugars.

3. Long, narrow <u>body</u> cells carry messages throughout your body.

4. In <u>meiosis</u>, body cells divide producing two new cells with identical nuclei.

5. A <u>gene</u> is the cell that results when an egg cell and a sperm cell join.

6. Organisms that form during <u>asexual</u> reproduction inherit traits from both parents.

7. An <u>evolution</u> is an inherited trait that helps an organism to survive in its environment.

8. A <u>learned behavior</u> is a quick reaction to a stimulus.

9. <u>Food webs</u> are models that show how energy is used in an ecosystem.

10. A <u>desert</u> is a biome with high yearly temperatures and about 200 cm of rainfall.

Interpreting Data

The following chart shows the number of chromosomes found in the nucleus of a body cell of different species.

Animal	No. of chromosomes in nucleus of body cells
Housefly	12
Bullfrog	26
Rabbit	44
Human	46
Chicken	78
Crayfish	200

1. How many chromosomes are contained in the sperm or egg cell of a chicken?

2. How many chromosomes would the body cells of an unborn rabbit have?

3. What relationship appears to exist between the size or complexity of an animal and the number of chromosomes contained in its body cells?

Communicating Science

1. Draw and label a diagram comparing the major parts of plant and animal cells.

2. Write a paragraph explaining when and with what result cells undergo mitosis and meiosis.

3. Make a table showing several examples of physiological adaptations, structural adaptations, and behavioral adaptations.

4. Draw and label a diagram showing how pollution can affect the carbon dioxide-oxygen and nitrogen cycles.

Applying Science

1. Write a paragraph explaining why members of a family have some characteristics that are similar and some that are different.

2. Write copy for a brochure explaining why antibiotics shouldn't be overused. Explain how bacteria can become resistant to the antibiotics through natural selection.

Unit A
Performance Review

Life Science Convention

Using what you learned in this unit, help prepare exhibits and presentations for a Life Science Convention to be held at your school. Complete one or more of the following activities. You may work by yourself or in a group.

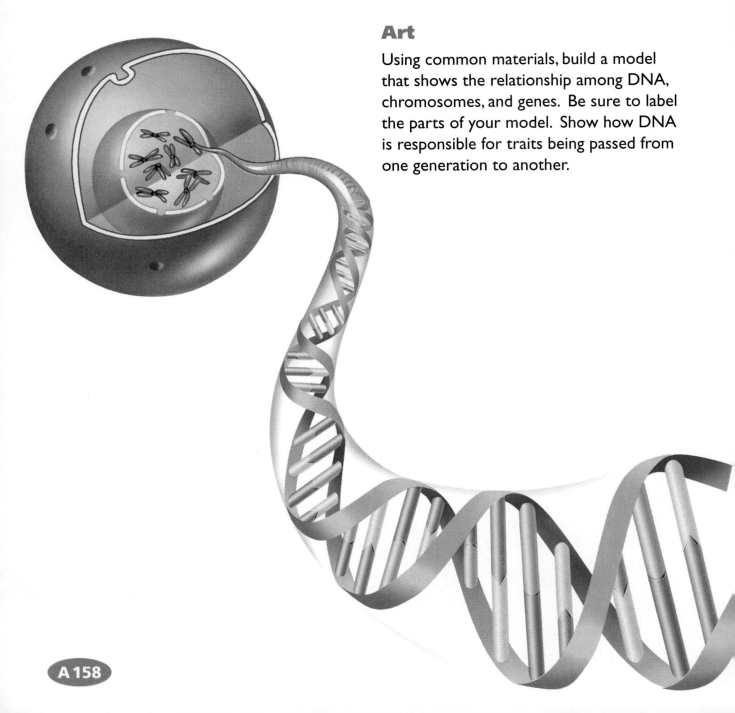

Art

Using common materials, build a model that shows the relationship among DNA, chromosomes, and genes. Be sure to label the parts of your model. Show how DNA is responsible for traits being passed from one generation to another.

Variety of Life

Prepare a display showing the variety of species of organisms. Include a microscopic display with prepared slides of different microscopic organisms. If possible, include different types of microscopes. Be prepared to explain to visitors what they are seeing.

Mathematics

Prepare a display board on sickle cell anemia, showing how you can predict the chances of children inheriting sickled cells from their parents. Include tables showing what happens when one parent has genes for normal and sickled cells and when both parents have genes for normal and sickled cells.

Environment

Work with other students to present a panel describing why the rainforests are disappearing and how this affects the environment, both locally and globally. Have each student on the panel talk about a different topic. Allow time for questions after the presentation.

Drama

In 1962, James Watson, Maurice Wilkins, and Francis Crick shared the Nobel prize for their work explaining the structure of DNA. Plan a skit of the presentation ceremony. Have a presenter from the Nobel committee speak first, and then have Watson, Wilkins, and Crick explain their model and give their acceptance speeches.

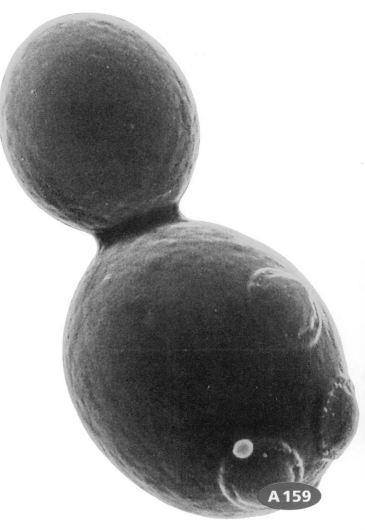

Using Graphic Organizers

A graphic organizer is a visual device that shows how ideas and concepts are related. There are many different kinds of graphic organizers. Word webs, flowcharts, and tables are a few examples.

Make a Graphic Organizer

In Chapter 1, you learned about the parts of cells. Use this information to make a graphic organizer. Your graphic organizer should show how cell parts can be used to classify plant and animal cells. Use the graphic organizer below to get you started.

Write Descriptive Paragraphs

Use your completed graphic organizer to write a three-paragraph description of cells and their parts. Your first paragraph should include an introduction and discuss parts that are present in all cells. Your second paragraph should discuss parts found only in plant cells. Your third paragraph should include a description of parts found only in animal cells and a summary of your writing.

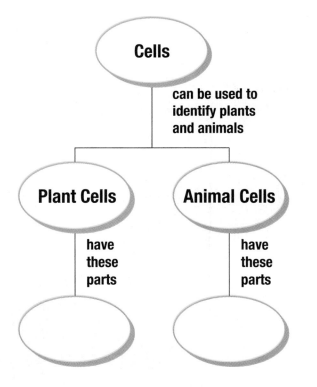

Remember to:

1. **Prewrite** Organize your thoughts before you write.

2. **Draft** Write your description.

3. **Revise** Share your work and then make changes.

4. **Edit** Proofread for mistakes and fix them.

5. **Publish** Share your description with your class.

Your Science Handbook

Safety in Science

Scientists know they must work safely when doing experiments. You need to be careful when doing experiments too. Here are some safety tips to remember.

Safety Tips

- Read each experiment carefully.
- Wear safety goggles when needed.
- Clean up spills right away.
- Never taste or smell substances unless directed to do so by your teacher.
- Handle sharp items carefully.
- Tape sharp edges of materials.
- Handle thermometers carefully.
- Use chemicals carefully.
- Dispose of chemicals properly.
- Put materials away when you finish an experiment.
- Wash your hands after each experiment.

Using the Metric System

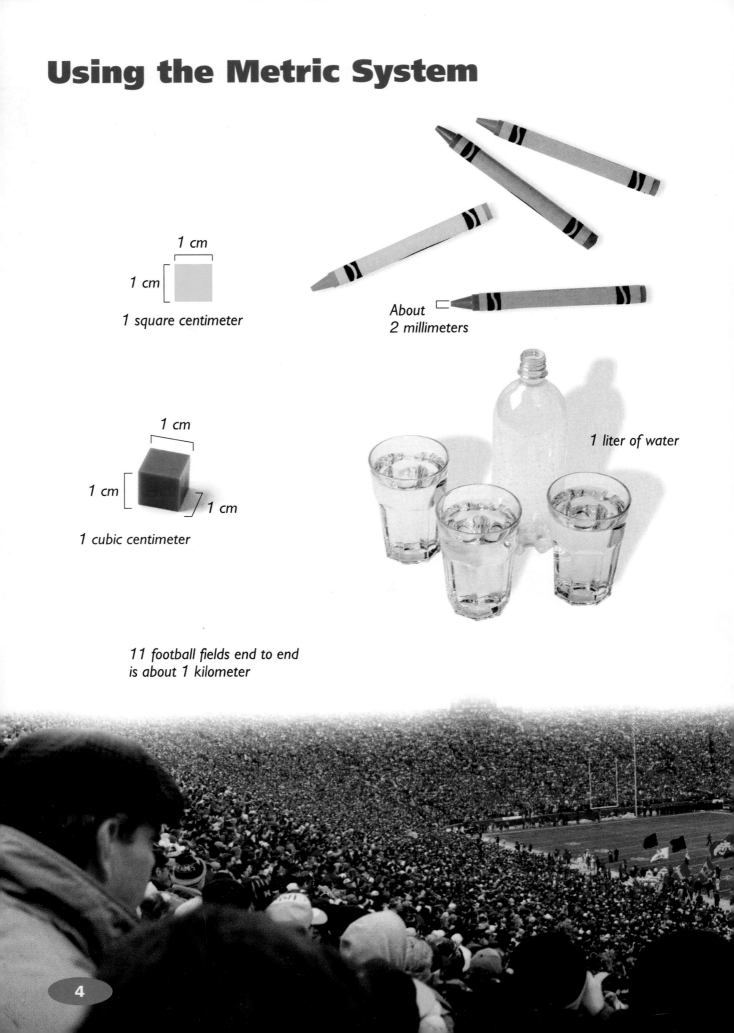

1 cm
1 cm
1 square centimeter

About 2 millimeters

1 cm
1 cm
1 cm
1 cubic centimeter

1 liter of water

11 football fields end to end is about 1 kilometer

4

About 1 centimeter

About 1 kilogram

Water boils
(100° C)

Normal body
temperature (37° C)

Water freezes
(0° C)

About 1
meter

Observing

How can you increase your powers of observation?

Using your senses helps you understand and learn about the world around you. For example, imagine picking up a ball. Think about the texture. Is it soft, hard, or a combination of both of these things? Does smelling the ball tell you if it is made of plastic or rubber? Imagine shaking it. Is it solid or hollow? Can you tell if something is inside the ball? Are there any characteristics about the ball that can help you determine whether or not the ball can bounce?

As a result of careful observations, you will understand how things and events change. This understanding allows you to make accurate comparisons. Every observation you make is an important one.

Practice Observing

Materials

- box of unshelled peanuts
- marker
- index card
- metric ruler
- hand lens

Follow This Procedure:

1. Choose a peanut from the box.

2. Use a marker to place a small identifying mark on the peanut. Do not share your mark with other students.

3. Observe your peanut carefully. Record as many observations about your peanut as you can on an index card. Be specific.

4. When you've finished observing your peanut, place it back into the box.

5. Exchange your observation card with a classmate. Use the observations on the cards to identify each other's peanuts.

Thinking About Your Thinking

What senses did you use to observe your peanut? Did your partner use observations similar to those you used? What additional observations could you have recorded to better describe your peanut?

Communicating

How can you communicate in an effective and easily understood way?

Good scientific communication uses words, pictures, charts, and graphs to give information that it is easily understood by people all around the world.

When you make and record observations, it is important to use exact words and to give as much information as possible. Compare the following observations that two students wrote after they observed the same experiment.

The liquid changed color and bubbles formed.

The liquid changed from pale yellow to bright red. Bubbles began forming almost immediately. The liquid bubbled rapidly for 27 seconds and then stopped.

The second student's observations are more exact and complete. Anyone reading these observations can get a fairly good idea of what the student observed. This is not true of the first student's description. The second student communicated in a more meaningful way.

Practice Communicating

Materials

- box of cards with pictures on them
- colored pencils
- 2 sheets of drawing paper

Follow This Procedure

1. Work with a partner. Choose a picture card from the box. Don't show the card to your partner.

2. Look at the picture on your card. Think how you would describe the picture to another person. Where would you start? What words would you use?

3. Slowly and carefully describe the picture on your card to your partner. As you describe the picture, your partner should draw what you describe.

4. When you've completed your description, compare your partner's drawing to the picture on the card. How well did you communicate what you saw?

5. Reverse roles and repeat steps 1–4.

Thinking About Your Thinking

What process did you use to describe your picture? What part did you describe first? Why did you decide to start with that part of the picture? How could you have communicated your information more clearly?

Classifying

How can you classify objects?

Classifying is the process of organizing or arranging objects into groups according to characteristics they share. You classify objects in order to organize your thoughts and knowledge about a subject. This organization of information helps you better understand the objects and events you observe.

What characteristics do the birds on this page share? Based on these similarities, the canary and the duck are both classified as birds. With this information, you can make generalizations about these animals based on your knowledge of the bird group. For example, you can conclude that the canary and the duck lay eggs because egg laying is a characteristic shared by all birds.

In order to classify objects, you must be able to recognize the characteristics that are similar or different among a group of objects. Then you can group the objects according to one or more of their similar characteristics.

Practice Classifying

Materials

- paper
- pencil
- buttons

Follow This Procedure:

1. Observe a group of buttons. Notice how the buttons are similar and how they are different. Record your observations on a sheet of paper.

2. Choose one characteristic. You might choose size, shape, color, or any other characteristic. Based on this characteristic, classify the buttons into two different groups. Record the characteristics each group shares.

3. Now classify each group into various smaller groups based on other similar characteristics. How are the buttons in each group similar? How are they different? Record the characteristics of each group.

4. Report your group's classification to the class. Discuss how the classifications differed among the groups.

Thinking About Your Thinking

The same objects can be classified differently by different people. Why do you think this might occur? Support your answer with some examples.

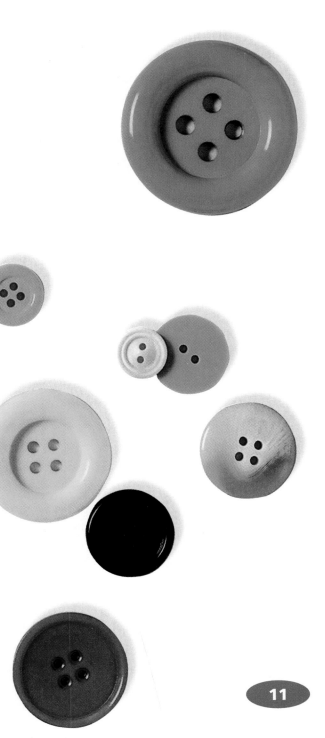

Estimating and Measuring

How can you accurately estimate and measure?

An estimate is an intelligent guess about an object or an event. One common characteristic that people estimate is measurement. As you get more practice measuring objects, you should find that making estimates that are very close to actual measurements becomes easier.

Being able to estimate volume is often helpful as you do science experiments. Estimating volume can be difficult if an object is irregularly shaped, such as the pebbles below. However, by finding the volume of one pebble, you can better estimate the volume of the other three.

Practice Estimating and Measuring

Materials
- 50-mL plastic graduated cylinder
- water
- 4 irregularly-shaped pebbles of varying sizes

Follow This Procedure

1 Copy the chart onto a sheet of paper. Use your chart to record your observations.

2 Fill a graduated cylinder with water to the 25-mL mark.

3 Choose the pebble that you think has the smallest volume.

4 Estimate the level to which you think the water will rise if you place the pebble into the cylinder. Record your estimate.

5 Gently place the pebble in the water. Record the level of the water in the cylinder.

6 Compare your estimate of the water level to the actual measurement. Are you surprised by the new water level?

7 Find the volume of the pebble by subtracting 25 mL from the actual level of water. Record this volume.

8 Repeat steps 4–7 until you have estimated and measured the volume of all four rocks.

Thinking About Your Thinking

Do you think it will be easier to predict the volume of a regularly-shaped object such as a marble than it is to predict the volume of an irregularly-shaped object? Why or why not?

Pebble	Estimated level of water	Actual level of water	Volume of pebble
1			
2			
3			
4			

Inferring

How can you make a valid inference?

When you make an inference, you make a reasonable guess about information that is not obvious. An inference is based on observations and past experience. In order to make an inference, you must make good observations and consider all the information you have about a situation. Think about how what you've observed relates to situations you are familiar with.

Inferring is an important first step toward predicting outcomes of experiments and forming testable hypotheses. Although an inference must be based on observations or facts, it doesn't always have to be true. After further investigation and experimentation, you might discover that your original inference missed the mark. If necessary, you can make another inference based on the new information you gathered.

Practice Inferring

Materials

- safety goggles
- spoon
- baking soda
- 3 small plastic cups
- hand lens
- dropper
- 3 unknown substances marked A, B, and C
- vinegar

Follow This Procedure

1. Copy the chart onto a sheet of paper. Use your chart to record your observations.

2. Put on your safety goggles. Place a half spoonful of baking soda in a plastic cup. Observe the baking soda with a hand lens. Record your observations.

3. Repeat step 2 with the unknown substances.

4. Make an inference. Based on your observations, which substances are baking soda? Record your inference on your paper.

5. Use the dropper to add three drops of vinegar to the cup with the baking soda. Observe what happens. Record your observations in your chart.

6. Repeat step 5 with Unknowns A–C.

7. Review your inferences from step 4. If necessary, make new inferences based on your observations.

Substance	Observations	
	Without Vinegar	With Vinegar
Baking soda		
Unknown A		
Unknown B		
Unknown C		

Thinking About Your Thinking

What information from this activity did you use to make your inferences? What information from past experiences did you use? How did making additional observations affect your inferences?

Predicting

How can you improve your predicting skills?

When you make a prediction, you guess what will happen in a particular situation. Your prediction is based on knowing what has happened in similar situations. The more information you have and the better your observations, the more likely you are to make accurate predictions.

Look at the cars and ramps below. What amount of force is needed to pull the car up the ramp in the first two pictures? How does this force relate to the height of the ramp?

Now, use the information from the first two photos to predict the amount of force needed to pull the car up the third ramp. Based on your observations of the first two pictures, you can predict that the force needed is three times that in the first picture, or 75N.

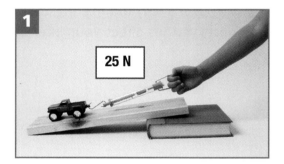

25 N

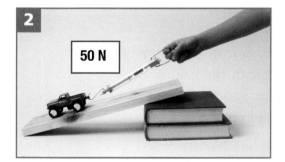

50 N

Practice Predicting

Materials

- feather
- book

Follow This Procedure:

1. Copy the chart onto a sheet of paper. Use your chart to record your predictions and observations.

2. Hold a book in one hand and a feather in the other. If you drop both at the same time, which will reach the ground first? Record your prediction in your chart.

3. Drop the two items. Record your results.

4. Place the feather on top of the book. If you drop the book with the feather lying on top, which will reach the ground first, the feather or the book? Record your prediction.

5. Drop the book with the feather on top of it. Record your results.

	Prediction	Observation
Feather and book dropped separately		
Book dropped with feather on top		

Thinking About Your Thinking

What information did you use to make your prediction in step 2? in step 4? What additional information would have helped you make better predictions?

17

Making Operational Definitions

How can you make an operational definition?

An operational definition is a definition or description of an object or an event based on the way you experience it.

An operational definition can describe many different qualities of an object or an event. It can explain what something does, what purpose something serves, or how an event takes place.

For example, look at the pictures below which show a strip of litmus paper that has been dipped into some vinegar. The pictures show that when the blue litmus paper is dipped into vinegar, which is an acid, it turns red. Based on this test, an operational definition for an acid might be "a substance that turns blue litmus paper red."

Practice Making Operational Definitions

Materials

- slice of potato
- paper towel
- dropper
- iodine solution
- slice of carrot
- small cup of water
- saltine
- piece of cooked egg white

Food Item	Starch?	Color when iodine is added
Potato	yes	
Carrot	yes	
Water	no	
Saltine	yes	
Egg white	no	

Follow This Procedure

1. Copy the chart onto a sheet of paper. Use your chart to record your observations.

2. Place a slice of potato on a paper towel.

3. With the dropper, place a small drop of iodine solution on the potato. Observe what happens to the potato. Record your observations in your chart.

4. Repeat steps 2 and 3 with the remaining food items.

5. Look up the definition for the word *starch* in a dictionary. Write the definition on your paper below your chart.

6. Look in the chart to see which items contain starch. Use that information and the results of this activity to write an operational definition of a starch.

Thinking About Your Thinking

How is your operational definition different from the definition of a starch in the dictionary? When might your operational definition be more useful than the dictionary definition?

19

Making and Using Models

How do scientific models help you understand science?

A scientific model can be an object or an idea that shows how something that you can't observe directly looks or works. Using models allows you to better understand objects, events, or ideas. Good models can be used to explain what you know and to predict what will happen.

The picture shows a model of one kind of object that is too tiny to see—a methane molecule. Scientists use models of molecules to explain why atoms act as they do and to predict how substances will react chemically with each other.

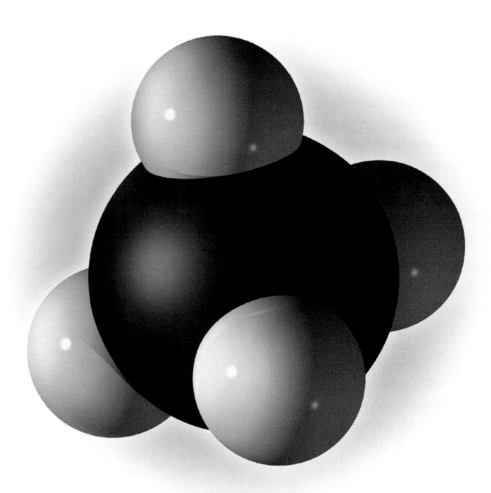

Methane Molecule

Practice Making and Using Models

Materials

- 2 different colors of clay
- toothpicks, broken in half

Follow This Procedure

1. Make a chart like the one shown. Use your chart to draw your molecules.

2. You will make clay models of molecules that contain hydrogen and oxygen atoms. Use one color of clay to make oxygen atoms for your model molecules. Use another color for hydrogen atoms.

3. Use the clay "atoms" to construct molecules of water, hydrogen peroxide, and hydrogen gas. The table shows how many atoms to include in each molecule and how the atoms are connected.

4. Complete the chart by making a drawing of your model.

Thinking About Your Thinking

How does having a physical model help you understand these molecules? Use your models to explain how the molecules of different substances vary.

Name	Atoms in one molecule	Arrangement	Drawing of molecule model
Water	2 hydrogen 1 oxygen	H⟍O⟋H	
Hydrogen peroxide	2 hydrogen 2 oxygen	H—O—O—H	
Hydrogen gas	2 hydrogen	H—H	

Formulating Questions and Hypotheses

Asking questions is an important part of the scientific process. Questions may come from a problem you have, from something you observe, or from things that interest you.

After you've identified a question, the next step is to formulate a hypothesis. Your hypothesis should be a clear statement that answers your question. A good hypothesis should also be testable. You should be able to design an experiment that would prove that your hypothesis is true or false.

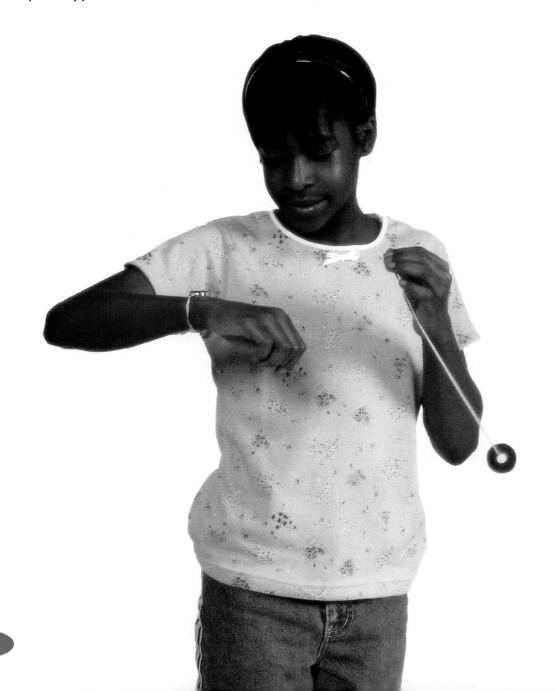

Practice Formulating Questions and Hypotheses

Materials

- scissors
- metric ruler
- string
- metal washer
- clock with a second hand

Follow This Procedure:

1 Make a chart like the one shown. Use your chart to record your data.

2 Cut and measure the length of a piece of string. Your string should be between 25 cm and 45 cm long. Record the length in your chart.

3 Tie a washer to one end of the string to make a pendulum.

4 Hold the washer out at about a 45° angle. This position is the start point for timing the period of the pendulum.

5 Release the washer. When the washer has swung back to the start point, one period has passed. Time how long it takes for 5 periods of the pendulum to occur. Record the time in your chart.

6 How do you think the length of the string affects the time it takes for one period? Write a hypothesis.

7 Test your hypothesis. Repeat steps 3–5 four more times, using a different length of string each time.

String length	Time for one period

Thinking About Your Thinking

On what information did you base your hypothesis? Did your data support your hypothesis? What other questions do you have as a result of this activity?

Collecting and Interpreting Data

How can you organize and interpret information that you collect?

When you make observations, you collect and interpret data. Arranging your data in graphs, tables, charts, or diagrams can make it easier to solve problems or answer questions. The best method of arranging your data depends on the type of data you collect and the way you plan to use it.

The graphics below display the same data in two different ways. Which graphic would you use to compare the growth of the two plants?

Plant Growth					
	Day 1	**Day 2**	**Day 3**	**Day 4**	**Day 5**
Plant in soil	3.0 cm	4.0 cm	4.5 cm	5.3 cm	6.0 cm
Plant in sand	3.0 cm	3.2 cm	3.6 cm	4.0 cm	4.1 cm

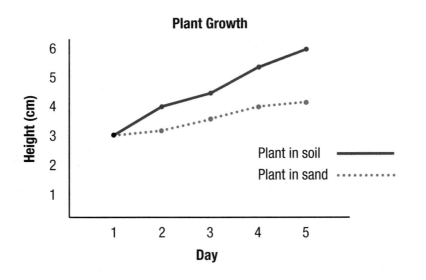

Practice Collecting and Interpreting Data

Follow This Procedure:

1 Work with a group. Collect the following data from each group member:

- How many people are in the person's family?

- What is the person's height?

- What color is the person's hair?

- What is the person's eye color

- How many years has the person lived in your city?

2 Decide with your group how to organize and display the data.

3 Discuss with your group how you would interpret these data. What might these data help you say about your group as a whole?

Thinking About Your Thinking

Why did you organize the data in the manner you chose? Could you present it in another way to emphasize a different view of your group? What other information would you add to your data to give a better picture of your group?

Identifying and Controlling Variables

How can you identify and control variables?

A variable is any factor that can change the outcome of an experiment. When you do experiments, it is important to identify and control variables. You do this by finding out which conditions make a difference in an experiment. To find how a particular variable affects the outcome of an experiment, you must control all other variables.

For example, suppose you wanted to find out whether more sugar dissolves in cold water or warm water. What variables would you control? What variable would change?

Practice Identifying and Controlling Variables

Materials

- measuring cup
- cold water
- 2 plastic cups
- 2 plastic spoons
- sugar
- very warm water

Follow This Procedure

1 Place 250 mL of cold water into a plastic cup.

2 Slowly add a half spoonful of sugar. Stir until all the sugar dissolves.

3 Keep adding sugar until no more will dissolve. Stir after each addition. Record the total amount of sugar you added to the cold water.

4 How much sugar will dissolve in very warm water? Decide how to test the warm water so that you can accurately compare it to the cold water. Decide on the following with your group as you develop a procedure to test the warm water.

- How much water should you use?
- How much sugar should you add at one time?
- Should you stir or not stir? If you stir, how long should you stir?

5 Use your procedure to test the warm water. Compare your results to those from the cold water.

Thinking About Your Thinking

How much warm water did you use? Why did you choose that amount? What variables did you control? Why?

Experimenting

How can you perform valuable experiments?

Scientific experiments test a hypothesis or attempt to solve a problem. The results of the investigation can be used to form a conclusion about the hypothesis or to state an answer to the problem.

First, state the problem you are investigating as a clear question and write a hypothesis. Then identify the variables that might affect the results of your investigation. Identify the variable you will change. Keep all other variables the same.

Next, design your experiment. Write down the steps that you will use.

When you do the experiment, record your data clearly so that other people can understand what you did and how you did it. Your results should always be reported honestly, even if they were different from what you expected.

Finally, interpret your data and state your conclusions.

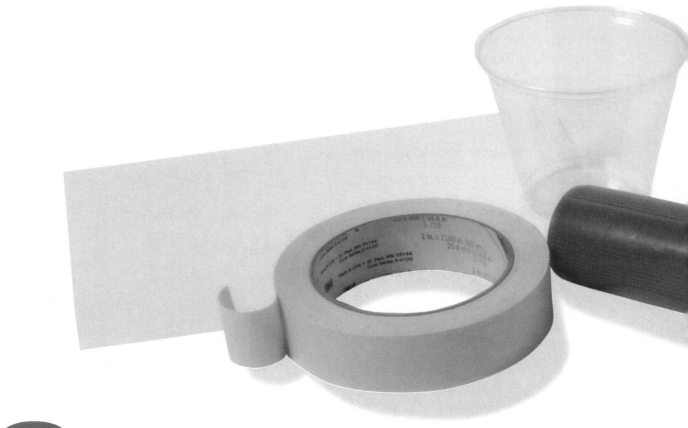

Practice Experimenting

Materials

- tape
- cup
- flashlight
- metric ruler

Follow This Procedure

1 Think about what you know about shadows. How does the distance between an object and a source of light affect the size of the object's shadow?

2 On a sheet of paper write a hypothesis to answer this question.

3 Design an experiment to test your hypotheses. Write a procedure. Use the materials in the materials list to do your experiment. Remember to identify and control the variables.

4 Make a chart to record your data.

5 Perform your experiment, following the steps in your procedure. Be sure to record your data.

6 Interpret your data and state your conclusion.

Thinking About Your Thinking

What is the difference between a hypothesis, as in step 2, and a conclusion, as in step 6? What information is your hypothesis based on? What information is your conclusion based on?

Classification of Living Things

Scientists classify different species of organisms into the five kingdoms you see below. All organisms that are now living or once lived can be placed into one of these kingdoms. Organisms within each kingdom share certain traits. Grouping organisms in this manner helps scientists learn more about them.

Kingdom	Monera	Protist	Fungi	Plant	Animal
Type of Cells	Prokaryotic	Eukaryotic	Eukaryotic	Eukaryotic	Eukaryotic
One-celled or Many-celled	One-celled	One-and many-celled	One-and many-celled	One-and many-celled	Many-celled
Movement	Some move	Some move	None move	None move	All move
Nutrition	Some make their own food. Others get it from other organisms.	Some make their own food. Others get it from other organisms.	All get food from other organisms.	All make their own food.	Eat plants or other animals.

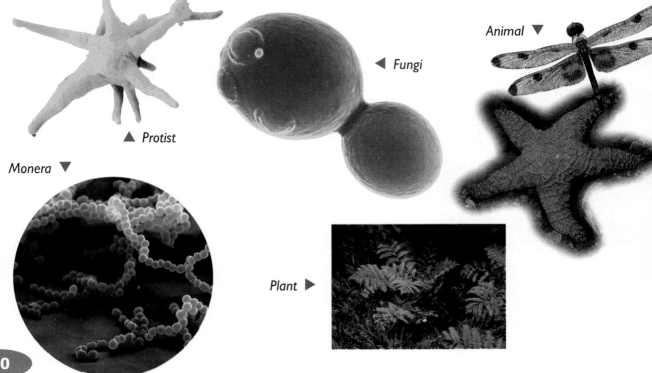

▲ Protist

◄ Fungi

Animal ▼

Monera ▼

Plant ▶

Circuits

Electric current can flow only when it can follow a complete circuit. In series circuits, the current has only one path it can follow. Current can travel in more than one path in a parallel circuit.

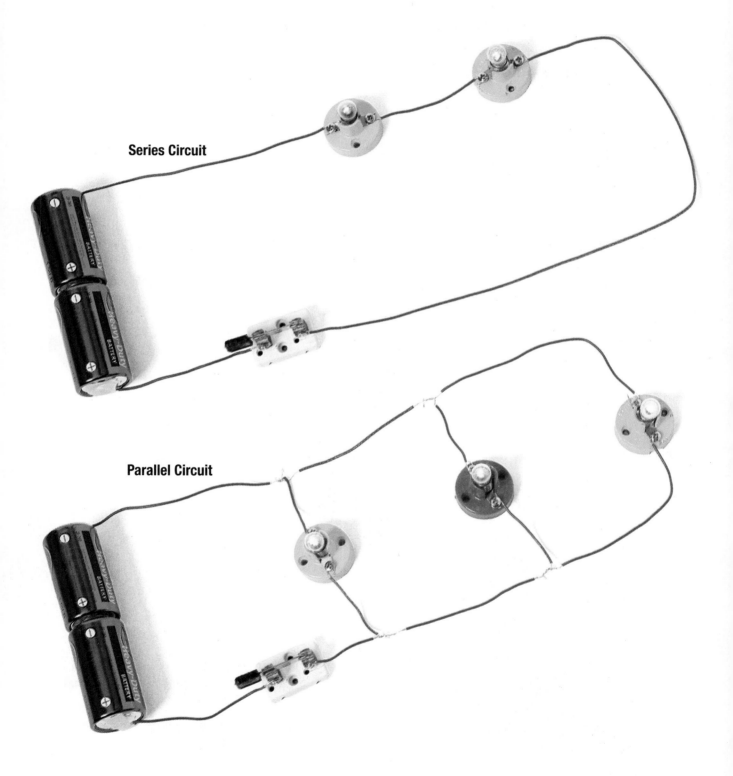

Series Circuit

Parallel Circuit

Energy in our World

The sun is the source of all energy on the earth. In fact, electromagnetic radiation of about 100 thousand million million joules reaches the earth from the sun each second. This energy is converted to different forms. You can follow some of these energy conversions in the pictures below.

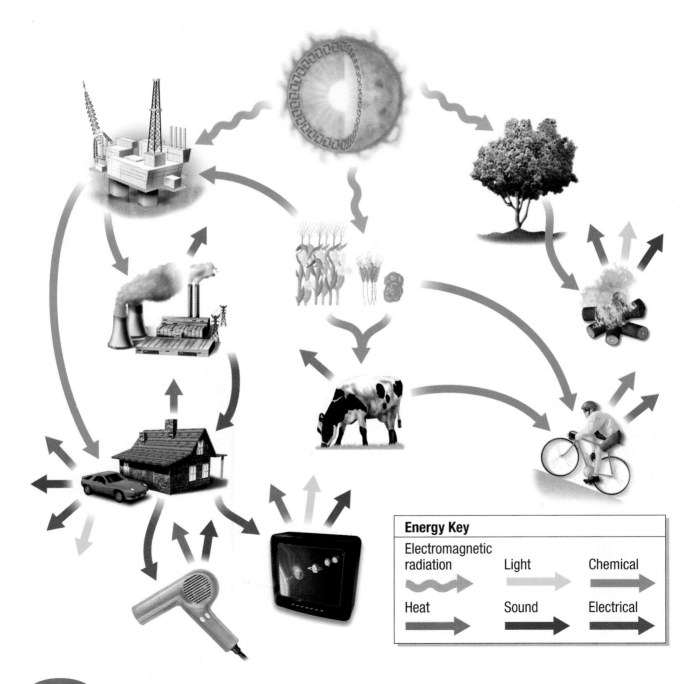

Energy Key

Electromagnetic radiation

Light

Chemical

Heat

Sound

Electrical

Simple Machines

Machines make work easier. Machines can be very simple, like the four simple machines shown on this page, or they can be complicated machines, such as automobiles.

Lever

Pulley

Wheel and Axle

Inclined Plane

Rock Cycle

Scientists classify rocks into three main types—igneous, metamorphic, and sedimentary. Each type of rock forms at least partly from other rocks. All rocks undergo continuous changes, which are brought about by heat, pressure, chemical reactions, or other forces that wear away or deposit materials. This change of rock from one type to another in a sequence is called the rock cycle.

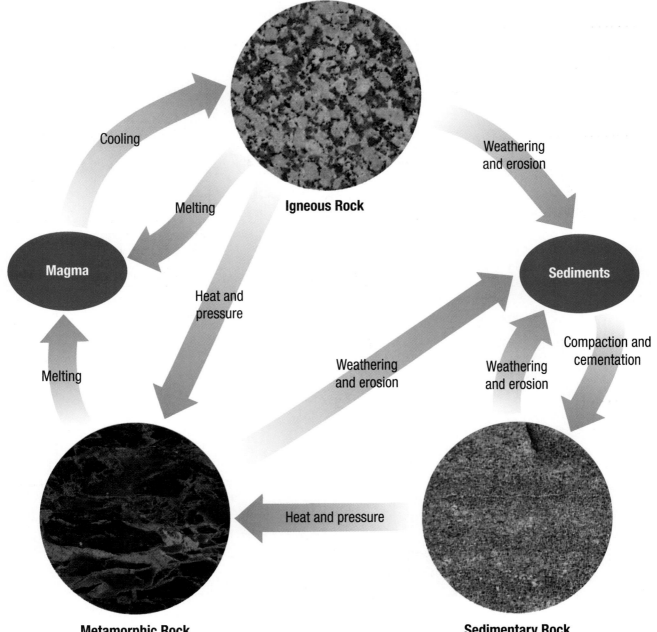

Cooling

Melting

Igneous Rock

Weathering and erosion

Magma

Heat and pressure

Sediments

Compaction and cementation

Melting

Weathering and erosion

Weathering and erosion

Heat and pressure

Metamorphic Rock

Sedimentary Rock

Characteristics of Planets

Planet	Mercury	Venus	Earth	Mars	Jupiter	Saturn	Uranus	Neptune	Pluto
Average distance to sun (AU)	0.387	0.723	1.000	1.524	5.203	9.529	19.191	30.061	39.529
Period of rotation days hours minutes	58 15 28	243 00 14	00 23 56	00 24 37	00 09 55	00 10 39	00 17 14	00 16 03	06 09 17
Period of revolution	87.97 days	224.70 days	365.26 days	686.98 days	11.86 years	29.46 years	84.04 years	164.79 years	248.53 years
Diameter	4,878	12,104	12,756	6,794	142,796	120,660	51,118	49,528	2,290
Mass (Earth=1)	0.06	0.82	1.00	0.11	317.83	95.15	14.54	17.23	0.002
Density (g/cm³)	5.42	5.24	5.50	3.94	1.31	0.70	1.30	1.66	2.03
Surface gravity (Earth=1)	0.38	0.90	1.00	0.38	2.53	1.07	0.92	1.12	0.06
Number of known satellites	0	0	1	2	16	18	15	8	1
Known rings	0	0	0	0	4	thousands	11	4	0

Layers of the Atmosphere

Earth's atmosphere extends thousands of kilometers above Earth's surface. The higher you go, the thinner the atmosphere becomes. You can see the four layers of the atmosphere below. The ionosphere is an area of the atmosphere that is made up of ions that reflect radio waves.

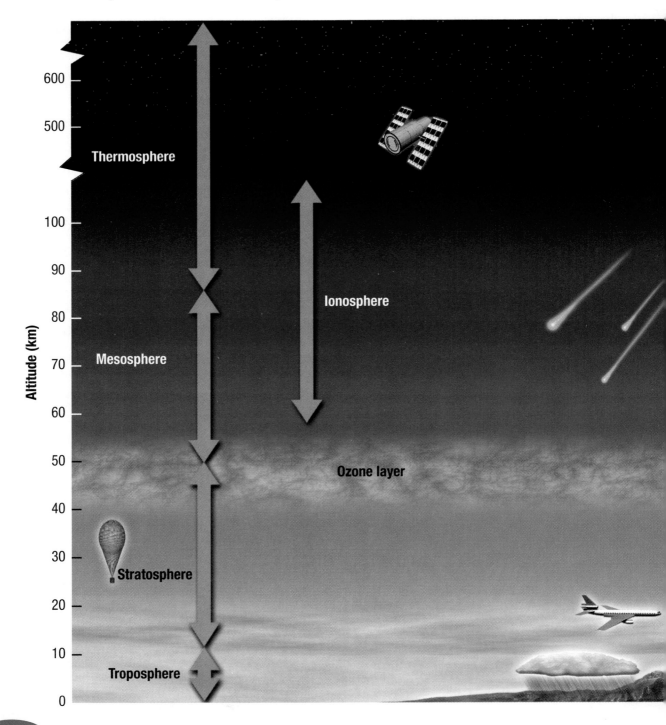

Atoms and Molecules

All matter is made of atoms, which are made of protons, neutrons, and electrons. Neutrons and protons form the nucleus of the atom. Electrons constantly change their positions as they travel around the nucleus. Atoms chemically combine to form a molecule.

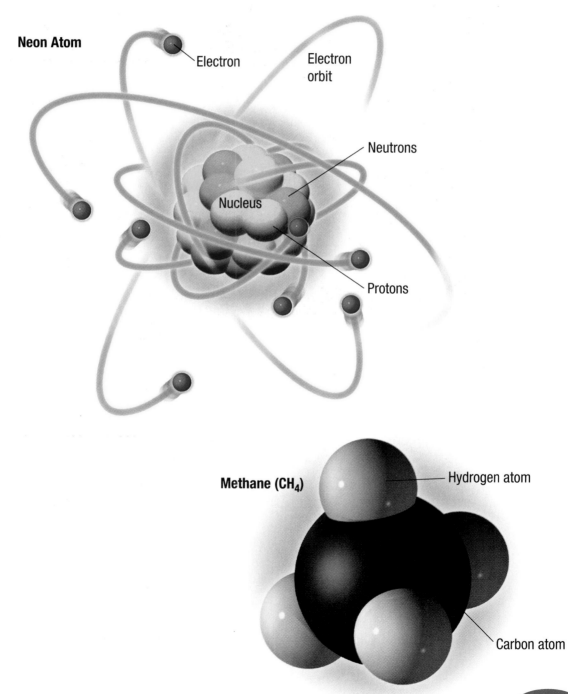

Neon Atom

Electron

Electron orbit

Neutrons

Nucleus

Protons

Methane (CH$_4$)

Hydrogen atom

Carbon atom

The Human Body

The different organs in your body make up organ systems. The parts of a simple system work together to perform a function. In a similar way, the organs in a system in your body work together to perform a function. All the systems work together to make your body work.

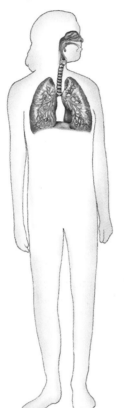

Respiratory System

◀ *Your respiratory system helps bring oxygen to the cells of your body and carries carbon dioxide and other wastes from cells. Air you breathe enters your lungs and passes into blood vessels that take it to all your cells.*

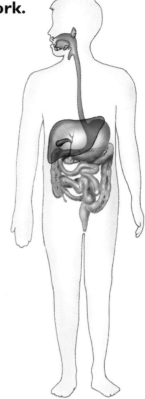

Digestive System

▲ *Organs in your digestive system break down food into nutrients that your cells can use. Some of the organs grind and mash the food. Others produce digestive fluids. Then blood vessels carry digested foods to all the cells of your body.*

Nervous System

◀ *Your nervous system includes your brain, spinal cord, and nerves. It gathers information from your environment, passes information to different parts of your body, and helps you interpret and use the information. Your brain sends signals to your muscles to let you move. Nerves send messages to and from other organs so they function properly.*

Circulatory System

Your heart, blood, and blood vessels make up your circulatory system. This system carries nutrients from your digestive system, oxygen brought in by your respiratory system, and wastes from both systems. These substances are transported to and from your body cells. ▶

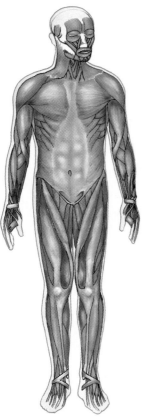

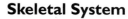

Muscular System

▲ *Many of the muscles in your body make up the muscular system. These muscles work with your bones to move the parts of your body. Nerves control the muscles. Blood vessels bring them the nutrients and oxygen they need to work.*

Skeletal System

◀ *All the bones in your body make up the skeletal system. They work together to protect and support your body and to help it move.*

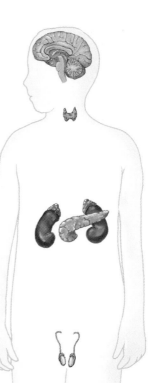

Endocrine System

◀ *The endocrine system is made up of glands that secrete hormones directly into the blood. These hormones control certain functions in your body.* ▶

Tools of Science

Scientists use a variety of tools. You too will use tools as you do science activities. Some of those tools are shown on these two pages.

Balance

▲ A balance is used to measure mass. To find the mass of an object, add standard masses to the pan opposite the object until the pans are balanced.

Graduated Cylinder

Graduated cylinders and beakers can be used to measure volume, or the amount of space an object takes up. ▶

Thermometer

◀ A thermometer is used to measure the temperature of an object. The liquid in the thermometer expands when it gets warmer and contracts when it cools. This causes the liquid to move up and down the temperature scale.

Spring Scale

◀ A spring scale is used to measure force. Because the weight of an object is a measure of the force of gravity on the object, you can use a spring scale to measure weight in grams.

Meterstick

A meterstick measures length in meters. It is divided into smaller units—usually centimeters and millimeters. ▼

Microscope

A microscope contains a series of lenses that make objects appear larger. By changing the combination of lenses, you can magnify objects by different amounts. ▶

Periodic Table of the Elements

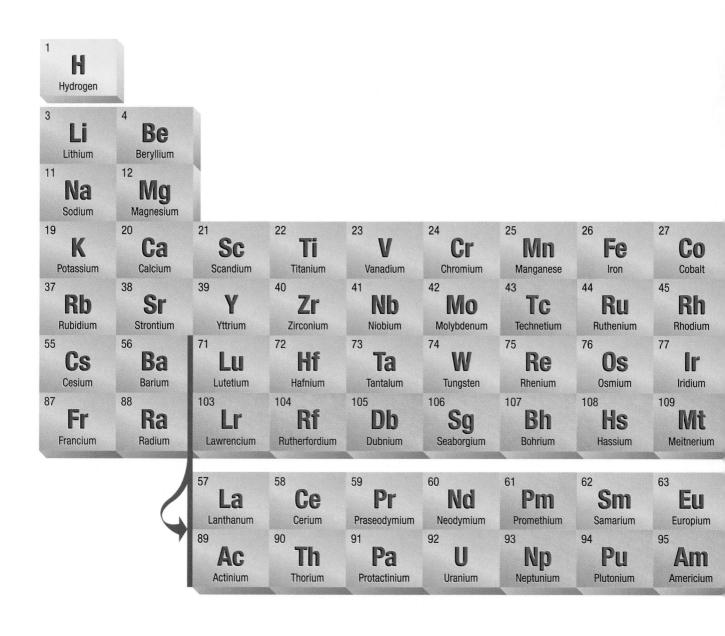

1 **H** Hydrogen								
3 **Li** Lithium	4 **Be** Beryllium							
11 **Na** Sodium	12 **Mg** Magnesium							
19 **K** Potassium	20 **Ca** Calcium	21 **Sc** Scandium	22 **Ti** Titanium	23 **V** Vanadium	24 **Cr** Chromium	25 **Mn** Manganese	26 **Fe** Iron	27 **Co** Cobalt
37 **Rb** Rubidium	38 **Sr** Strontium	39 **Y** Yttrium	40 **Zr** Zirconium	41 **Nb** Niobium	42 **Mo** Molybdenum	43 **Tc** Technetium	44 **Ru** Ruthenium	45 **Rh** Rhodium
55 **Cs** Cesium	56 **Ba** Barium	71 **Lu** Lutetium	72 **Hf** Hafnium	73 **Ta** Tantalum	74 **W** Tungsten	75 **Re** Rhenium	76 **Os** Osmium	77 **Ir** Iridium
87 **Fr** Francium	88 **Ra** Radium	103 **Lr** Lawrencium	104 **Rf** Rutherfordium	105 **Db** Dubnium	106 **Sg** Seaborgium	107 **Bh** Bohrium	108 **Hs** Hassium	109 **Mt** Meitnerium

57 **La** Lanthanum	58 **Ce** Cerium	59 **Pr** Praseodymium	60 **Nd** Neodymium	61 **Pm** Promethium	62 **Sm** Samarium	63 **Eu** Europium
89 **Ac** Actinium	90 **Th** Thorium	91 **Pa** Protactinium	92 **U** Uranium	93 **Np** Neptunium	94 **Pu** Plutonium	95 **Am** Americium

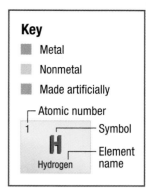

Key

■ Metal

■ Nonmetal

■ Made artificially

Atomic number

Symbol

Element name

1
H
Hydrogen

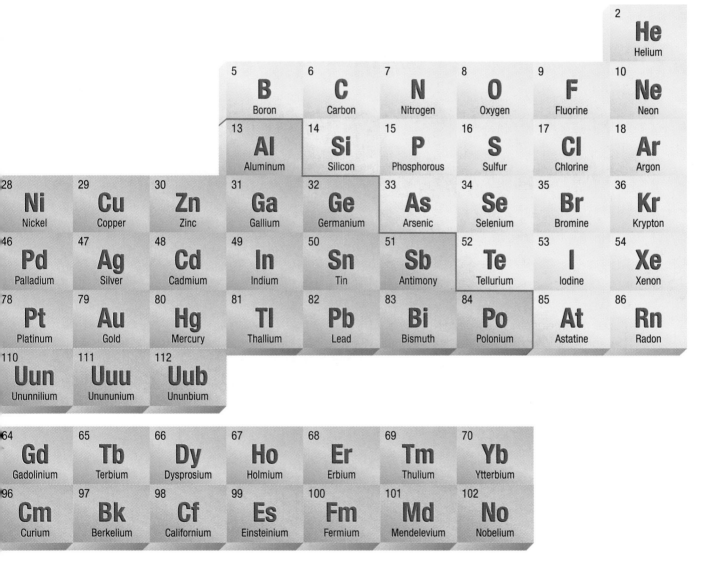

2 **He** Helium

| 5 **B** Boron | 6 **C** Carbon | 7 **N** Nitrogen | 8 **O** Oxygen | 9 **F** Fluorine | 10 **Ne** Neon |
| 13 **Al** Aluminum | 14 **Si** Silicon | 15 **P** Phosphorous | 16 **S** Sulfur | 17 **Cl** Chlorine | 18 **Ar** Argon |

28 **Ni** Nickel	29 **Cu** Copper	30 **Zn** Zinc	31 **Ga** Gallium	32 **Ge** Germanium	33 **As** Arsenic	34 **Se** Selenium	35 **Br** Bromine	36 **Kr** Krypton
46 **Pd** Palladium	47 **Ag** Silver	48 **Cd** Cadmium	49 **In** Indium	50 **Sn** Tin	51 **Sb** Antimony	52 **Te** Tellurium	53 **I** Iodine	54 **Xe** Xenon
78 **Pt** Platinum	79 **Au** Gold	80 **Hg** Mercury	81 **Tl** Thallium	82 **Pb** Lead	83 **Bi** Bismuth	84 **Po** Polonium	85 **At** Astatine	86 **Rn** Radon
110 **Uun** Ununnilium	111 **Uuu** Unununium	112 **Uub** Ununbium

| 64 **Gd** Gadolinium | 65 **Tb** Terbium | 66 **Dy** Dysprosium | 67 **Ho** Holmium | 68 **Er** Erbium | 69 **Tm** Thulium | 70 **Yb** Ytterbium |
| 96 **Cm** Curium | 97 **Bk** Berkelium | 98 **Cf** Californium | 99 **Es** Einsteinium | 100 **Fm** Fermium | 101 **Md** Mendelevium | 102 **No** Nobelium |

8000 B.C.	6000 B.C.	4000 B.C	2000 B.C.

Life Science

Physical Science

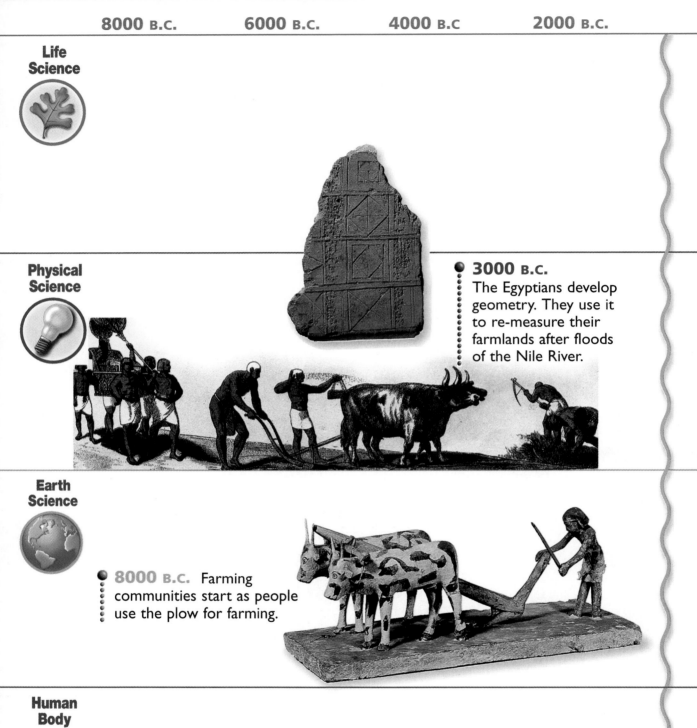

● **3000 B.C.**
The Egyptians develop geometry. They use it to re-measure their farmlands after floods of the Nile River.

Earth Science

● **8000 B.C.** Farming communities start as people use the plow for farming.

Human Body

4th century B.C.
Aristotle classifies
plants and animals.

3rd century B.C.
Aristarchus proposes that the
earth revolves around the sun.

4th century B.C.
Aristotle describes the
motions of falling
bodies. He believes that
heavier things fall faster
than lighter things.

260 B.C. Archimedes
discovers the principles of
buoyancy and the lever.

4th century B.C. Aristotle
describes the motions
of the planets.

200 B.C. Eratosthenes calculates
the size of the earth. His result is
very close to the earth's actual
size.

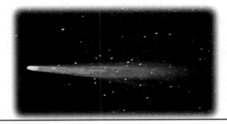

87 B.C.
Chinese report observing
an object in the sky that
later became known as
Halley's comet.

5th and 4th centuries B.C.
Hippocrates and other Greek
doctors record the symptoms of
many diseases. They also urge
people to eat a well-balanced diet.

**Life
Science**

**Physical
Science**

83 A.D.
Chinese travelers
use the compass
for navigation.

**About
750–1250**
Islamic scholars get
scientific books
from Europe. They
translate them into
Arabic and add
more information.

**Earth
Science**

140 Claudius Ptolemy
draws a complete picture of
an earth-centered universe.

132 The Chinese make the
first seismograph, a device
that measures the strength
of earthquakes.

**Human
Body**

2nd century Galen
writes about anatomy
and the causes of
diseases.

1100s
Animal guide books begin to appear. They describe what animals look like and give facts about them.

1250
Albert the Great describes plants and animals in his book *On Vegetables and On Animals.*

1555
Pierre Belon finds similarities between the skeletons of humans and birds.

9th century
The Chinese invent block printing. By the 11th century, they had movable type.

1019
Abu Arrayhan Muhammad ibn Ahmad al'Biruni observed both a solar and lunar eclipse within a few months of each other.

1543
Nikolaus Copernicus publishes his book *On The Revolutions of the Celestial Orbs*. It says that the sun remains still and the earth moves in a circle around it.

1265
Nasir al-Din al-Tusi gets his own observatory. His ideas about how the planets move will influence Nikolaus Copernicus.

About 1000
Ibn Sina writes an encyclopedia of medical knowledge. For many years, doctors will use this as their main source of medical knowledge. Arab scientist Ibn Al-Haytham gives the first detailed explanation of how we see and how light forms images in our eyes.

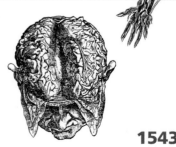

1543
Andreas Vesalius publishes *On the Makeup of the Human Body*. In this book he gives very detailed pictures of human anatomy.

47

1600	1620	1640	1660	1680

Life Science

1663 Robert Hooke first sees the cells of living organisms through a microscope. Antoni van Leeuwenhoek discovers bacteria with the microscope in 1674.

1679 Maria Sibylla Merian paints the first detailed pictures of a caterpillar turning into a butterfly. She also develops new techniques for printing pictures.

Physical Science

1600 William Gilbert describes the behavior of magnets. He also shows that the attraction of a compass needle toward North is due to the earth's magnetic pole.

1632 Galileo Galilei shows that all objects fall at the same speed. Galileo also shows that all matter has inertia.

1687 Isaac Newton introduces his three laws of motion.

Earth Science

1609–1619 Johannes Kepler introduces the three laws of planetary motion.

1610 Galileo uses a telescope to see the rings around the planet Saturn and the moons of Jupiter.

1669 Nicolaus Steno sets forth the basic principles of how to date rock layers.

1650 Maria Cunitz publishes a new set of tables to help astronomers find the positions of the planets and stars.

1693–1698 Maria Eimmart draws 250 pictures depicting the phases of the moon. She also paints flowers and insects.

1687 Isaac Newton introduces the concept of gravity.

Human Body

1628 William Harvey shows how the heart circulates blood through the blood vessels.

1735 Carolus Linnaeus devises the modern system of naming living things.

1704 Isaac Newton publishes his views on optics. He shows that white light contains many colors.

1759 Emile du Châtelet translates Isaac Newton's work into French. Her work still remains the only French translation.

1789 Antoine-Laurent Lavoisier claims that certain substances, such as oxygen, hydrogen, and nitrogen, cannot be broken down into anything simpler. He calls these substances "elements."

1729 Stephen Gray shows that electricity flows in a straight path from one place to another.

1781 Caroline and William Herschel (sister and brother) discover the planet Uranus.

1784 French chemist Antoine-Laurent Lavoisier does the first extensive study of respiration.

1798 Edward Jenner reports the first successful vaccination for smallpox.

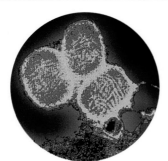

1721 Onesimus introduces to America the African method for inoculation against smallpox.

49

| 1805 | 1810 | 1815 | 1820 | 1825 | 1830 | 1835 |

Life Science

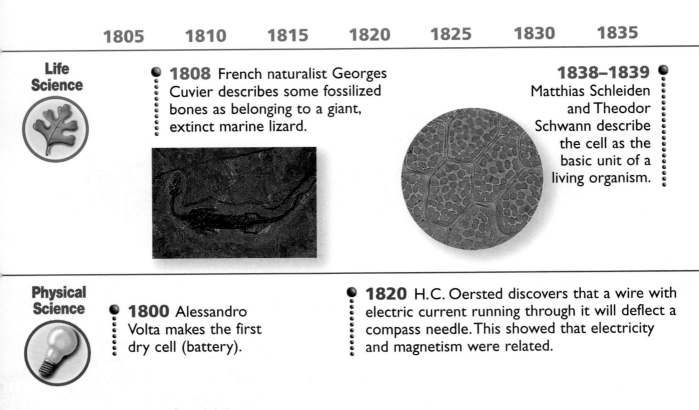

1808 French naturalist Georges Cuvier describes some fossilized bones as belonging to a giant, extinct marine lizard.

1838–1839 Matthias Schleiden and Theodor Schwann describe the cell as the basic unit of a living organism.

Physical Science

1800 Alessandro Volta makes the first dry cell (battery).

1820 H.C. Oersted discovers that a wire with electric current running through it will deflect a compass needle. This showed that electricity and magnetism were related.

1808 John Dalton proposes that all matter is made of atoms.

Earth Science

1830 Charles Lyell writes *Principles of Geology*. This is the first modern geology textbook.

1803 Luke Howard assigns to clouds the basic names that we still use today— cumulus, stratus, and cirrus.

Human Body

1842 Richard Owen gives the name "dinosaurs" to the extinct giant lizards.

1859 Charles Darwin proposes the theory of evolution by natural selection.

1863 Gregor Mendel shows that certain traits in peas are passed to succeeding generations in a regular fashion. He outlines the methods of heredity.

1847 Hermann Helmholtz states the law of conservation of energy. This law holds that energy cannot be created or destroyed. Energy only can be changed from one form to another.

1842 Christian Doppler explains why a car, train, plane, or any quickly moving object sounds higher pitched as it approaches and lower pitched as it moves away.

1866 Ernst Haeckel proposes the term "ecology" for the study of the environment.

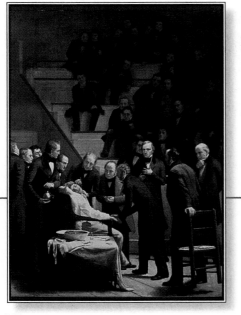

Early 1860s Louis Pasteur realizes that tiny organisms cause wine and milk to turn sour. He shows that heating the liquids kills these germs. This process is called pasteurization.

1840s Doctors use anesthetic drugs to put their patients to sleep.

1850s and 1860s Ignaz P. Semmelweis and Sir Joseph Lister pioneer the use of antiseptics in medicine.

Life Science

1900–1910 George Washington Carver, the son of slave parents, develops many new uses for old crops. He finds a way to make soybeans into rubber, cotton into road-paving material, and peanuts into paper.

Physical Science

1897 J. J. Thomson discovers the electron.

1905 Albert Einstein introduces the theory of relativity.

1895 Wilhelm Roentgen discovers X rays.

1896 Henri Becquerel discovers radioactivity.

Earth Science

1907 Bertram Boltwood introduces the idea of "radioactive" dating. This allows geologists to accurately measure the age of a fossil.

1912 Alfred Wegener proposes the theory of continental drift. This theory says that all land on the earth was once a single mass. It eventually broke apart and the continents slowly drifted away from each other.

Human Body

1885 Louis Pasteur gives the first vaccination for rabies. Pasteur thought that tiny organisms caused most diseases.

1920s Ernest Everett Just performs important research into how cells metabolize food.

1947 Archaeologist Mary Leakey unearths the skull of a *Proconsul africanus,* an example of a fossilized ape.

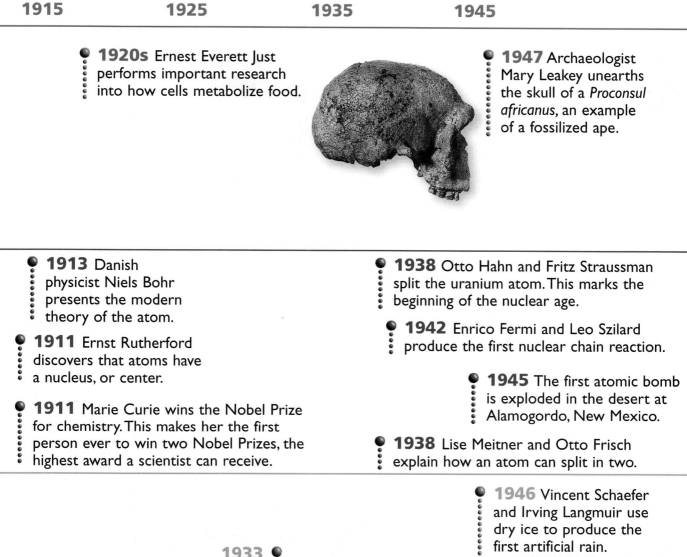

1913 Danish physicist Niels Bohr presents the modern theory of the atom.

1911 Ernst Rutherford discovers that atoms have a nucleus, or center.

1911 Marie Curie wins the Nobel Prize for chemistry. This makes her the first person ever to win two Nobel Prizes, the highest award a scientist can receive.

1938 Otto Hahn and Fritz Straussman split the uranium atom. This marks the beginning of the nuclear age.

1942 Enrico Fermi and Leo Szilard produce the first nuclear chain reaction.

1945 The first atomic bomb is exploded in the desert at Alamogordo, New Mexico.

1938 Lise Meitner and Otto Frisch explain how an atom can split in two.

1946 Vincent Schaefer and Irving Langmuir use dry ice to produce the first artificial rain.

1933 Meteorologist Tor Bergeron explains how raindrops form in clouds.

1917 Florence Sabin becomes the first woman professor at an American medical college.

1928 Alexander Fleming notices that the molds in his petri dish produced a substance, later called an antibiotic, that killed bacteria. He calls this substance penicillin.

1935 Chemist Percy Julian develops physostigmine, a drug used to fight the eye disease glaucoma.

1922 Doctors inject the first diabetes patient with insulin.

Life Science

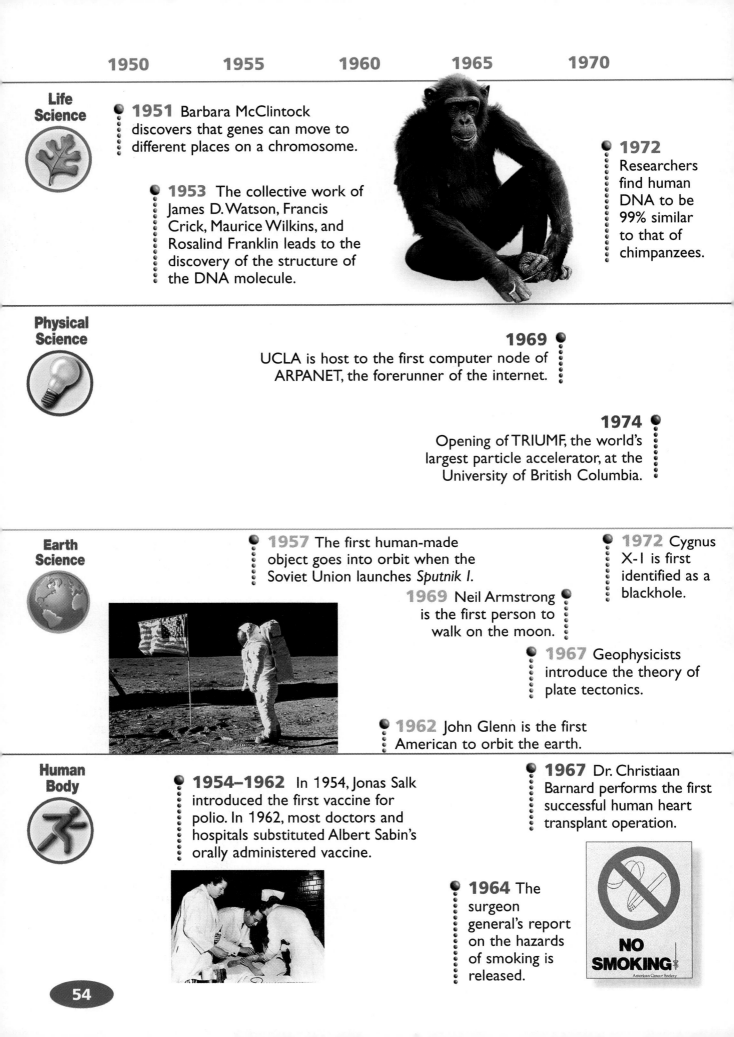

1951 Barbara McClintock discovers that genes can move to different places on a chromosome.

1953 The collective work of James D. Watson, Francis Crick, Maurice Wilkins, and Rosalind Franklin leads to the discovery of the structure of the DNA molecule.

1972 Researchers find human DNA to be 99% similar to that of chimpanzees.

Physical Science

1969 UCLA is host to the first computer node of ARPANET, the forerunner of the internet.

1974 Opening of TRIUMF, the world's largest particle accelerator, at the University of British Columbia.

Earth Science

1957 The first human-made object goes into orbit when the Soviet Union launches *Sputnik I*.

1969 Neil Armstrong is the first person to walk on the moon.

1972 Cygnus X-1 is first identified as a blackhole.

1967 Geophysicists introduce the theory of plate tectonics.

1962 John Glenn is the first American to orbit the earth.

Human Body

1954–1962 In 1954, Jonas Salk introduced the first vaccine for polio. In 1962, most doctors and hospitals substituted Albert Sabin's orally administered vaccine.

1967 Dr. Christiaan Barnard performs the first successful human heart transplant operation.

1964 The surgeon general's report on the hazards of smoking is released.

NO SMOKING
American Cancer Society

| 1975 | 1980 | 1985 | 1990 | 1995 | 2000 |

1988 ●
Congress approves funding for the Human Genome Project. This project will map and sequence the human genetic code.

1997 ●
Scientists in Edinburgh, Scotland, successfully clone a sheep, Dolly.

1975 The first personal computer goes for sale: The Altair.

1996 Scientists make "element 112" in the laboratory. This is the heaviest element yet created.

1979 A near meltdown occurs at the Three Mile Island nuclear power plant in Pennsylvania. This alerts the nation to the dangers of nuclear power.

1976 National Academy of Sciences reports on the dangers of chlorofluorocarbons (CFCs) for the earth's ozone layer.

1995 The first "extra-solar" planet is discovered.

Early 1990s The National Severe Storms Laboratory develops NEXRAD, the national network of Doppler weather radar stations for early severe storm warnings.

1981 The first commercial Magnetic Resonance Imaging scanners are available. Doctors use MRI scanners to look at the non-bony parts of the body.

1982 Dr. Stanley Prusiner identifies a new kind of disease-causing agent—prions. Prions are responsible for many brain disorders.

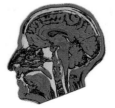

1998 John Glenn, age 77, orbits the earth aboard the space shuttle *Discovery*. Glenn is the oldest person to fly in space.

Glossary

Full Pronunciation Key

The pronunciation of each word is shown just after the word, in this way: **ab·bre·vi·ate** (ə brē′vē āt).

The letters and signs used are pronounced as in the words below.

The mark ′ is placed after a syllable with primary or heavy accent, as in the example above.

The mark ′ after a syllable shows a secondary or lighter accent, as in **ab·bre·vi·a·tion** (ə brē′vē ā′shən).

a	hat, cap	g	go, bag	ō	open, go	ŦH	then,	zh	measure,
ā	age, face	h	he, how	ò	all, caught		smooth		seizure
â	care, fair	i	it, pin	ô	order	u	cup, butter		
ä	father, far	ī	ice, five	oi	oil, voice	ù	full, put	ə	represents:
b	bad, rob	j	jam, enjoy	ou	house, out	ü	rule, move		a in about
ch	child, much	k	kind, seek	p	paper, cup	v	very, save		e in taken
d	did, red	l	land, coal	r	run, try	w	will,		i in pencil
e	let, best	m	me, am	s	say, yes		woman		o in lemon
ē	equal, be	n	no, in	sh	she, rush	y	young, yet		u in circus
ėr	term, learn	ng	long, bring	t	tell, it	z	zero,		
f	fat, if	o	hot, rock	th	thin, both		breeze		

A

acceleration (ak sel′ə rā′shən), the change in velocity during a particular time period.

acid (a′sid), a compound that releases hydrogen ions in water.

adaptation (ad′ap tā′shən), an inherited trait that helps a species survive in its environment.

addiction (ə dik′shən), a disease affecting both the mind and body that makes people unable to go without something, such as a drug.

air mass (er mas), a large body of air having similar properties or weather conditions.

air pressure (er presh′ər), the force of air against Earth's surface.

air resistance (er ri zis′təns), the friction from air molecules hitting an object as the object moves through the air.

alcohol (al′kə hòl), depressant drug found in beer, wine, and liquor.

alcoholic (al′kə hò lik), a person who does not have control over his or her drinking.

alcoholism (al′kə hò liz′əm), a disease in which a person is unable to stop abusing alcohol.

alternative energy sources
(òl tėr′nə tiv en ər jē sôrs), source of energy other than fossil fuels.

amplitude (am′plə tüd), the distance between a wave's midpoint and its crest or trough.

anemometer (an′ə mom′ə tər), an instrument used to measure wind speed.

aquifer (ak′wə fər), a layer of rock in which ground water can accumulate and flow freely.

asexual reproduction (ā sek′shü əl rē prə duk′shən), reproduction by one parent.

auroras (ô ror′əz), the glow or display of lights in the skies near polar latitudes.

axon (ak′son), part of a neuron that carries messages away from the cell body.

B

balanced forces (bal′enst fôrs′əs), equal forces acting in opposite directions.

barometer (bə rom′ə tər), an instrument used to measure air pressure.

base (bās), a compound that releases hydroxide ions when dissolved in water.

base (bās), one kind of molecule that makes up a DNA strand.

behavioral adaptation (bi hā′vyər əl ad′ap tā′shən), an action that aids survival.

big bang theory (big bang thē′ar ē), the idea that the universe started with a huge explosion about 15 billion years ago.

biome (bī′ōm), large geographic region with a particular kind of climate and community.

black hole (blak hōl), an invisible object in space whose mass and gravitational force is so great that not even light can escape.

brain stem (brān stem), part of the brain that controls involuntary actions, such as breathing; connects the brain to the spinal cord.

C

caffeine (kaf′ēn), a mild stimulant found in coffee, tea, colas, and chocolate.

carbon monoxide (kär′bən mo nok′sīd), a gas found in cigarette smoke that replaces some of the blood's oxygen when inhaled.

carnivore (kär′nə vôr), a consumer that eats only animals.

cell division (sel də vizh′ən), the dividing of a cell following mitosis.

cell membrane (sel mem′brān), thin outer covering that holds a cell together.

cell theory (sel thē′ər ē), theory stating that the cell is the basic unit of all living organisms, and only living cells can produce new living cells.

cell wall (sel wôl), tough, nonliving material that acts like an outside skeleton for each plant cell.

central nervous system (sen′trəl nėr′vəs sis′təm), part of the nervous system made up of the brain and spinal cord.

cerebellum (ser′ə bel′əm), part of the brain that coordinates movements and helps maintain balance.

cerebrum (sə rē′brəm), part of the brain that controls thinking and voluntary movements and receives information from the senses.

chemical equation (kem′ə kel i kwā′zhən), an arrangement of symbols and formulas used to show what happens during a chemical reaction.

chlorophyll (klôr′ə fil), green substance in chloroplasts that traps energy from sunlight.

chloroplast (klôr′ə plast), organelle that makes sugars, using carbon dioxide, water, and the energy from sunlight.

chromosome (kro′mə sōm), stringlike structure in a cell nucleus that carries information controlling all the cell's activities.

competition (kom′pə tish′ən), a situation in which two or more organisms attempt to use the same resource.

compound microscope (kom′pound mī′krə skōp), microscope having more than one lens.

compressional wave (kəm presh′ən əl wāv), wave in which matter vibrates in the same direction as the energy waves traveling through it.

concave mirror (kon kāv′ mir′ər), a mirror whose center curves away from an object.

concentrated (kon′sən trā′tid), describes a solution with a large amount of solute compared to the amount of solvent.

condensation (kon′den sā′shən), the change of state from a gas to a liquid.

conservation (kon′sər vā′shən), careful use of resources so they will last longer.

convex mirror (con veks′ mir′ər), a mirror whose center curves toward an object.

corona (kə rō′nə), a crown of glowing gases around the sun that can be seen during a total solar eclipse.

cytoplasm (sī′tə plaz′əm), clear, jellylike material that fills the space between the cell membrane and the nucleus.

D

dendrite (den′drīt), part of a neuron that collects information from other neurons.

depressant (di pres′nt), a drug that slows down the nervous system.

dew point (dü point), the temperature at which a volume of air cannot hold any more water vapor.

dilute (dī lüt′), describes a solution with a small amount of solute compared to the amount of solvent.

displacement (dis plās′mənt), the direction and shortest distance traveled during a change of position.

distance (dis′təns), the total length of the path between two points.

DNA (dē en ā), the molecule in each cell that directs the cell's activities.

dominant gene (dom′ə nənt jēn), a gene that prevents the expression of another gene.

Doppler radar (dop′lər rā′där), a type of radar that calculates distance and shows direction of movement.

drainage basin (drā′nij bā sin), the land area from which a river system gets its water.

drug (drug), a substance that acts on the body to change the way it works.

drug abuse (drug ə byüz), using drugs for purposes other than health.

E

endocrine gland (en′dō krən gland), a tissue or organ that releases chemical substances into the bloodstream.

endocrine system (en′dō krən sis′təm), body system consisting of glands, hormones, and target cells that work together to control various functions in the body.

endoplasmic reticulum (en′dō plaz′mik ri tik′yə ləm), organelle that transports materials inside the cell.

endothermic reaction (en′dō thèr′mik rē ak′shən), a chemical reaction in which more energy is taken in than given off.

energy pyramid (en′ər Jē pir′ə mid), a model that shows how energy is used in a food chain or an ecosystem.

equinox (ē′kwə noks), a point in the Earth's orbit around the sun where nights and days are the same length.

estuary (es′chü er′ē), place where fresh water from rivers or streams mixes with saltwater from the ocean.

evaporation (i vap′ə rā′shən), the change of a state from liquid to gas at the surface of a liquid.

evolution (ev′ə lü shən), process that results in changes in the genetic makeup of a species over very long periods of time.

exothermic reaction (ek′sō thér′mik rē ak′shən), a chemical reaction in which more energy is given off than is taken in.

F

fault (fôlt), a crack in the earth's crust along which rock moves.

fertilization (fèr′tl ə zā′shən), the joining of an egg cell and a sperm cell during sexual reproduction.

focal point (fō′kəl point), the point at which light rays meet when reflected or refracted.

focus (fō′kəs), the point along a fault where rock first breaks or moves, causing an earthquake.

force (fôrs), a push or a pull.

forecast (fôr′kast′), a prediction of what the weather will be like in the near future.

formula (fôr′myə lə), arrangement of symbols that shows both the kinds and number of atoms in a compound.

fossil fuel (fos′əl fyü′əl), fuel such as coal, natural gas, and oil that formed underground millions of years ago from decaying organic matter.

frame of reference (frām ov ref′ər əns), the object an observer uses to detect motion.

frequency (frē′kwən sē), the number or waves (crests or troughs) that pass a point in a given amount of time.

freshwater biome (fresh′wō′tər bī′ōm), water biome that has a low salt content.

friction (frik′shən), a force between surfaces that resists the movement of one surface past the other surface.

front (frunt), the boundary between warm and cold air masses.

fusion (fyü′zhen), the combining of less massive elements to form more massive elements.

G

galaxy (gal′ək sē), a system of billions of stars, gases, and dust.

gene (jēn), a section of DNA on a chromosome that controls a trait.

geologic time scale (jē ə loj′ik tīm skāl), a record of Earth's history based on events interpreted from the rock record and fossil evidence.

glacier (glā′shər), a large mass of moving ice.

gravity (grav′ə tē), the force of attraction that exists between any two objects.

groundwater (ground wô′tər), water in the ground near the Earth's surface.

H

hallucinogen (hə lü′sn ə jen), drug that affects brain activity, changing the way a person senses the world.

herbivore (hér′bə vôr), a consumer that eats plants or other producers.

heredity (hə red′ə tē), the process by which traits are passed from parents to offspring.

hormone (hôr′mōn), chemicals released by endocrine glands that cause target cells to perform specific activities.

humidity (hyü mid′ə tē), water vapor in the air.

hurricane (hėr′ə kān), a large tropical storm that forms over warm oceans and whose winds have a velocity of at least 110 kilometers per hour.

hybrid (hī′brid), an organism with one dominant and one recessive gene for a trait.

hypothalamus (hī′pō thal′ ə məs), part of the brain that controls body temperature, hunger, thirst, and emotions.

I

index fossil (in′deks fos′əl), a fossil of an organism that existed on Earth for a short time over a large geographic area.

indicator (in′də kā′tər), a substance that changes color at a certain range of pH values.

inertia (in ėr′shə), the resistance of an object to change in its state of motion.

inhalant (in hā′lənt), drug that enters your body with the air you breathe.

inherit (in her′it), to receive from one's mother or father.

instantaneous speed (in′stən tā′nē əs spēd), the speed at any given point.

instinct (in′stingkt), an inherited behavior.

intensity (in ten′sə tē), a measure of the amount of energy in a wave.

intoxicated (in tok′sə kā′tid), experiencing the symptoms of heavy alcohol consumption.

L

laser light (lā′zer līt), light of a single wavelength with all the waves lined up.

law (lȯ), a statement that describes events or relationships that exist in nature.

lithosphere (lith′ə sfir), the solid rocky outer layer of the earth that includes the crust.

lunar eclipse (lü′nər i klips′), a darkening of the moon when it passes through Earth's shadow.

M

mass (mas), the amount of matter in an object.

meiosis (mī ō′sis), the process by which sex cells form.

meteorologist (mē′tē ə rol′ə jist), scientist who studies the weather.

mitochondria (mī′tə kon′drē ə), organelles where food and oxygen react to release energy.

mitosis (mī tō′sis), the process by which a cell produces two new identical nuclei.

moraine (mə rān′), a ridge formed when a glacier deposits its sediments.

motor neuron (mō′tər nür′on), nerve cell in the peripheral nervous system that carries information from the central nervous system to muscles and organs.

music (myü′zik), pleasant sound with regular wave patterns.

mutation (myü tā′shən), a permanent change in DNA that occurs when DNA copies itself.

N

natural selection (nach′ər əl si lek′shən), the idea that those organisms best adapted to their environment will be the ones most likely to survive and reproduce.

nebula (neb′yə lə), cloud of dust and gas in space.

nerve impulse (nėrv im′puls), message that travels from the dendrites of a neuron to the axon.

net force (net fôrs), the combination of all the forces acting on an object.

neuron (nür′on), a nerve cell.

neutralization (nü′trə li zās′shən), a process in which an acid and a base react to produce a salt and water.

newton (nüt′n), in the metric system, the unit used to measure force or weight.

nicotine (nik′ə tēn), a stimulant drug found in tobacco.

noise (noiz), sound with no regular wave patterns.

nonrenewable resource (non′ri nü′ə bəl ri sôrs′), a resource that cannot be replaced.

nucleus (nü′klē əs), part of the cell that controls activities of other cell parts.

O

octave (ok′tiv), a musical sequence in which the top note has twice the frequency of the bottom note.

omnivore (om′ni vôr), a consumer that eats both producers and consumers.

opaque (ō pāk′), does not allow light to pass through.

ore (ôr), a rock that contains enough of a mineral to be of value.

organelle (or/gə nel/), tiny structure in the cytoplasm of a cell that performs a special job.

P

peripheral nervous system (pə rif/ər əl nėr/vəs sis/təm), part of the nervous system that connects the central nervous system with all other parts of the body.

permafrost (pėr/mə frôst/), ground that is permanently frozen.

pH scale (pē āch skāl), a set of numbers between 0 and 14 to measure the strength of acids and bases.

photon (fō/ton), a bundle of energy that is released when an atom loses some energy.

physiological adaptation (fiz/ē ə loj/ə kəl ad/ap tā/shən), adaptation that involves a body part's job of controlling a life process.

plankton (plangk/tən), microscopic, free-floating organisms that serve as food for larger organisms.

plate tectonics (plāt tek ton/iks), theory that states that the lithosphere is broken into plates that move.

pollutant (pə lüt/nt), harmful substance in the environment.

population (pop/yə lā/shən), all the organisms of one species that live in a certain place.

product (prod/əkt), a substance that is formed in a chemical reaction.

psychrometer (sī krom/ə tər), an instrument used to measure relative humidity.

purebred (pyür/bred/), an organism with two dominant or two recessive genes for a trait.

Q

quasar (kwā/sär), brilliant object in space that may be the powerhouses of developing galaxies.

R

reactant (rē ak/tənt), a substance that undergoes a chemical reaction, often by combining with another substance.

recessive gene (re ses/iv jēn), a gene whose expression is prevented by a dominant gene.

red giant (red jī/ənt), a star that has swelled and glows with a red color.

red shift (red shift), the change of light waves from retreating objects to the red end of the spectrum.

reflex (rē/fleks), quick, automatic response to a stimulus.

refraction (ri frak/shən), the bending of a light wave as it moves from one material to another.

relative humidity (rel/ə tiv hyü mid/ə tē), measurement that compares the amount of water vapor in the air with the amount air can hold at a certain temperature.

relative motion (rel/ə tiv mō/shən), the change in position of one object compared to the position of another.

renewable resource (ri nü/ə bəl ri sôrs/), a resource that can be replaced within a reasonably short time.

reservoir (rez′ər vwär), artificial lake used to collect and store water.

respiration (res′pə rā′shən), energy-producing process in which a cell combines oxygen with sugars and gives off carbon dioxide and water.

response (ri spons′), a reaction of an organism to a change in the environment.

retina (ret′nə), an area at the back of the eye that contains sensory receptors for light.

ribosome (ri′bə sōm), organelle that puts together proteins for the cell.

Richter scale (rik′tər skāl), a scale used to compare the strengths of earthquakes.

S

saltwater biome (sôlt′wô′tər bī′ōm) water biome that has high salt content.

sediment (sed′ə mənt), rock and soil carried by water.

seismograph (sīz′mə graf), instrument that records the strengths of the earth's movements, based on the amount of energy released.

sensory neuron (sen′sər ē nür′on), nerve cell in the peripheral nervous system that carries information from sensory receptors to the CNS.

sensory receptor (sen′sər ē ri sep′tər), cell within the peripheral nervous system that gathers information from the environment and from the inside of the body.

sex cell (seks sel), a type of cell produced only by an organism that reproduces sexually.

sexual reproduction (sek′shü əl rē prə duk′shən), reproduction by two parents.

side effect (sīd ə fekt′), unwanted effect of a medicine or drug.

smokeless tobacco (smōk′lis tə bak′ō), tobacco, such as chewing tobacco or snuff, that is not smoked when it is used.

soil profile (soil prō′fīl), layers of soil in an area.

solar eclipse (sō′lər i klips′), an alignment of the sun, moon, and Earth where the moon blocks the sun from Earth's view.

solar energy (sō′lər en ər jē), radiant energy that comes from the sun.

solar flare (sō′lər fler), powerful eruption of very hot gases from the sun.

solstice (sol′stis), a point in the Earth's orbit around the sun where daylight is either the longest or shortest amount possible.

solute (sol′yüt), a substance that is dissolved.

solvent (sol′vənt), a substance that dissolves other materials.

sonar (sō′när), a device that uses sound waves to measure distance.

species (spē′shēz), a group of organisms that have the same characteristics and are able to produce offspring that can reproduce.

speed (spēd), the distance an object moves in a certain period of time.

speedometer (spē dom′ə tər), a device that shows instantaneous speed.

spinal cord (spī′nl kord), bundle of neurons that carries messages back and forth between the brain and the rest of the body.

stewardship (stü′ərd ship), the taking care of Earth's resources to ensure their quality and quantity for future generations.

stimulant (stim′yōō lənt), a drug that speeds up the nervous system.

stimulus (stim′yə ləs), a change in the environment of an organism that causes a response.

structural adaptation (struk′cher əl ad′ap tā′shən), adaptation that involves body parts or color.

sunspot (sun′spot′), a region on the sun of very strong magnetic fields.

supernova (sü′pər nō′və), the explosion of a star, releasing huge amounts of light and other energy.

synapse (si naps′), the gap between the axon of one neuron and the dendrite of a second neuron.

T

taiga (tī′gə), forest biome just south of the tundra, characterized by conifers.

tar (tär), a sticky, gluelike substance found in cigarette smoke.

tides (tīdz), the rise and fall of water in the ocean and seas caused mainly by the gravitational pull of the moon on the earth.

tornado (tôr nā′dō), a violent, funnel-shaped cloud with extremely strong winds.

trait (trāt), a characteristic of an organism.

transparent (tran spər′ənt), allows light to pass through so that objects on the other side can be seen.

transverse wave (trans vėrs′ wāv), a wave in which the crests and troughs move at right angles to the direction of the wave's travel.

tundra (tun′drə), the northernmost and coldest biome.

V

vacuole (vak′yü ōl), saclike organelle used for storing materials.

velocity (və los′ə tē), a measure of both the speed and direction of a moving object.

vent (vent), opening on the ocean floor.

W

water table (wô′tər tā′bəl), the top of an aquifer.

weathering (weᴛʜ′ər ing), group of processes that break rocks into smaller pieces.

weight (wāt), a measure of the pull of gravity on an object's mass.

Z

zygote (zī′gōt), the first cell of an offspring, formed when an egg cell and sperm cell join.

Index

Acknowledgments

Illustration
Borders Patti Green
Icons Precison Graphics

Unit A
8a John Zielinski
17 Carla Kiwior
19 Christine D. Young
21 Christine D. Young
22 Precision Graphics
41 Barbara Cousins
44 Vilma Ortiz-Dillon
47 Barbara Cousins
53 Barbara Cousins
54 Barbara Cousins
56 Barbara Cousins
58a Barbara Cousins
59 John Zielinski
63 Barbara Cousins
64 Richard Stergulz
65 Richard Stergulz
78 Barbara Harmon
82 Richard Stergulz
84 Precision Graphics
88 Carla Kiwior
90 Walter Stuart
91 Walter Stuart
114 Meryl Treatner
119 Carla Kiwior
120 Michael Digiorgio
121 Michael Digiorgio
124b Precision Graphics
126a Precision Graphics
128 Precision Graphics
130a Carla Kiwior
137a Precision Graphics
137b Michael Carroll
137c Michael Carroll
138 Precision Graphics
149 Carla Kiwior
150 Carla Kiwior
151 Carla Kiwior
152 Carla Kiwior
158 Barbara Cousins, Steven Edsey & Sons.

Unit B
12 Rob Schuster
15 J/B Woolsey
17 Michael Carroll
23 George Hamblin
34 J/B Woolsey
36 J/B Woolsey
38 J/B Woolsey
40 J/B Woolsey
44 J/B Woolsey
51 J/B Woolsey
58 Kenneth Batelman
65 Dave Merrill
86 John Massie
89 Kenneth Batelman
90 Walter Stuart
93 Precision Graphics
99 J/B Woolsey
107 Pedro Gonzalez
120 Kenneth Batelman
121 George Hamblin
122 J/B Woolsey
123 J/B Woolsey
124 J/B Woolsey
125 J/B Woolsey
127 J/B Woolsey
135 Kenneth Batelman
136 Kenneth Batelman
137 Michael Carroll
141 J/B Woolsey
142 J/B Woolsey
143 Michael Carroll
145 John Massie
147 Michael Carroll
150 Michael Carroll
151 Kenneth Batelman

Unit C
8 Kenneth Batelman
11 J/B Woolsey
12 Jared Schneidman
13 J/B Woolsey
14 Precision Graphics
16 Precision Graphics
21 John Zielinski
23 Michael Carroll
28 Precision Graphics
31 Precision Graphics
33 Precision Graphics
45a Precision Graphics
45b Nadine Sokol
47 Alan Cormack
48 George Hamblin
49 Alan Cormack
55 J/B Woolsey
58 J/B Woolsey
59 J/B Woolsey
60 Michael Carroll
62 Carla Kiwior
64 Precision Graphics
70 Nadine Sokol
71 Michael Digiorgio
72 Carla Kiwior
74 Precision Graphics
82 J/B Woolsey
84 J/B Woolsey
85 J/B Woolsey
86 J/B Woolsey
88 J/B Woolsey
89 J/B Woolsey
92 J/B Woolsey
94 J/B Woolsey
96 J/B Woolsey
100 John Zielinski
119 Precision Graphics
122 Michael Digiorgio
131 J/B Woolsey
133 Precision Graphics
143 J/B Woolsey

Unit D
9 Joel Ito
11 Rodd Ambroson
14 Rodd Ambroson
15 Rodd Ambroson
16 Rodd Ambroson
20 Christine D. Young
23 Joel Ito
24 Joel Ito
45 Joel Ito
52 Joel Ito

Photography
Unless otherwise credited, all photographs are the property of Scott Foresman, a division of Pearson Education. Page abbreviations are as follows: (T) top, (C) center, (B) bottom, (L) left, (R) right, (INS) inset.

Cover: Roda/Natural Selection Stock Photography, Inc.

iv BR M. Abbey/Visuals Unlimited
v TR Joe McDonald/Animals Animals/Earth Scenes
ix TR PhotoDisc, Inc

Unit A
1 Kenneth Edward/Photo Researchers
2 T Vincent O'Bryne/Panoramic Images
2 B-inset-2 Mark C. Burnett/Photo Researchers
2 C Dan McCoy/Rainbow
2 B Arie deZanger for Scott Foresman
2 B-inset 1 Photo Researchers
3 B J. F. Podevin/Image Bank
3 TCR NASA/SPL/Photo Researchers
3 BCR G. I. Bernard/Animals Animals/Earth Scenes
9 C Eddy Gray/SPL/SSC/Photo Researchers
9 BL Rod Planck/TOM STACK & ASSOCIATES
9 TR Steven David Miller/Animals Animals/Earth Scenes
9 BR Mike Bacon/TOM STACK & ASSOCIATES
9 TL Bruce Watkins/Animals Animals/Earth Scenes
10 B Cecil Fox/SS/Photo Researchers
10 T Science VU/Visuals Unlimited
12 T Jan Hinsch/SPL/SSC/Photo Researchers
12 B David Parker/SPL/SSC/Photo Researchers
12 C Andrew Syred/SPL/SSC/Photo Researchers
13 T Mike Abbey/Visuals Unlimited
13 B Anthony Bannister/Animals Animals/Earth Scenes
16 Profesors P. Motta & T. Naguro/SPL/SSC/Photo Researchers
18 Professor P. Motta/Dept. of Anatomy/University "La Sapienza", Rome/SPL/SSC/Photo Researchers
20 M. Eichelberger/Visuals Unlimited
23 T Superstock, Inc.
23 B S. Maslowski/Visuals Unlimited
26 B Ray Coleman/NASC/Photo Researchers
26 T John D. Cunningham/Visuals Unlimited
27 TL David M. Phillips/Visuals Unlimited
27 TR Superstock, Inc.
27 BL Oliver Meckes/Ottawa/SPL/SSC/Photo Researchers
27 BR Professors P. M. Andrews/K.R. Porter and J. Vial/SSC/Photo Researchers
28 CL M. Abbey/Visuals Unlimited
28 BL Stan Flegler/Visuals Unlimited
28 BR Cabisco/Visuals Unlimited
29 B Malcolm Boulton/Photo Researchers
29 T Gopal Murti/CNRI/Phototake
30 T Profesor P. Motta/Dept. of Anatomy/University "La Sapienza", Rome/SPL/SSC/Photo Researchers
30 B K. Aufderheide/Visuals Unlimited
35 S. Maslowski/Visuals Unlimited
40 David M. Phillips/Visuals Unlimited
42 T Scott Brenner/Ken IWagner/Visuals Unlimited
42 B PhotoDisc, Inc.
43 T Dr. E. R. Degginger/Color-Pic, Inc.
43 B David M. Phillips/Visuals Unlimited
44 BL J. Forsdyke/Gene Cox/SPL/Photo Researchers
44 BC Biophoto Associates/Photo Researchers
44 BR Biophoto Associates/Photo Researchers
44 T Oliver Meckes/Photo Researchers
45 R Biophoto Associates/Photo Researchers
45 L Biophoto Associates/Photo Researchers
46 David M. Phillips/Photo Researchers
48 BL VU/Cabisco/Visuals Unlimited
48 BR VU/Cabisco/Visuals Unlimited
49 T Chris Johns/Tony Stone Images
49 BL VU/Cabisco/Visuals Unlimited
49 BR VU/Cabisco/Visuals Unlimited
50 T PhotoDisc, Inc.
50 B G. Thomas Bishop/Custom Medical Stock Photo
52 M. P. Kahl/Photo Researchers
58 BR David Parker/SPL/Photo Researchers
62 Walter Hodges/Tony Stone Images
62 Background PhotoDisc, Inc.
67 T Joe McDonald/Visuals Unlimited
67 B Alex Kerstitch/Visuals Unlimited
71 Chris Johns/Tony Stone Images
75 L Lynn Stone/Animals Animals/Earth Scenes
75 C Leonard Lee Rue III/Photo Researchers
75 R Francois Gohier/Photo Researchers
76 Jeff Lepore/Photo Researchers
77 T Francois Gohier/Photo Researchers
77 B Michael Fogden/Animals Animals/Earth Scenes
77 C Anthony Bannister/Animals Animals/Earth Scenes
79 L Lynn Stone/Animals Animals/Earth Scenes
79 R Francois Gohier/Photo Researchers
79 C Leonard Lee Rue III/Photo Researchers
80 Don W. Fawcett/Visuals Unlimited
81 B J. Koivula/SS/Photo Researchers

81 C Joe McDonald/Animals Animals/Earth Scenes
81 T James L. Amos/Photo Researchers
85 T Ken Lucas/Visuals Unlimited
85 B Michael Dick/Animals Animals/Earth Scenes
86 The Granger Collection, New York
86 Background MetaPhotos
87 BR J.W. Verderber/Visuals Unlimited
87 TR Hal Beral/Visuals Unlimited
87 TL Alex Kerstitch/Visuals Unlimited
89 T Breck P. Kent/Animals Animals/Earth Scenes
92 L Jan L. Wassink/Visuals Unlimited
92 R David C. Fritts/Animals Animals/Earth Scenes
94 T James Watt/Animals Animals/Earth Scenes
94 B PhotoDisc, Inc.
95 T C. P. Hickman/Visuals Unlimited
95 C E. R. Degginger/Animals Animals/Earth Scenes
95 B Chris McLaughlin/Animals Animals/Earth Scenes
96 B Howard Hall/OSF/Animals Animals/Earth Scenes
96 T Andrew Syred/SPL/Photo Researchers
97 B Adrienne T. Gibson/Animals Animals/Earth Scenes
97 T M. Abbey/Visuals Unlimited
100 Fred Bruemmer
101 T Jonathan Blair/National Geographic Image Collection
101 B J. Alcock/Visuals Unlimited
101 C N. M. Collins/OSF/Animals Animals/Earth Scenes
102 L Lee F. Snyder/Photo Researchers
102 R Francis Lepine/Animals Animals/Earth Scenes
103 T J. A. L. Cooke/Animals Animals/Earth Scenes
104 Charles Gupton/Tony Stone Images
105 Alfred B. Thomas/Animals Animals/Earth Scenes
109 Lee F. Snyder/Photo Researchers
113 T PhotoDisc, Inc.
113 TC Rod Planck/Photo Researchers
113 BC J. H. Robinson/Photo Researchers
113 B Renee Lynn/Photo Researchers
116 E. R. Degginger/Color-Pic, Inc.
117 B WHOI/D.Foster/Visuals Unlimited
117 T Stanley Flegler/Visuals Unlimited
118 B Renee Lynn/Photo Researchers
118 BC J. H. Robinson/Photo Researchers
118 TC Rod Planck/Photo Researchers
118 T PhotoDisc, Inc.
126 Oliver Meckes/Photo Researchers
127 Cabisco/Visuals Unlimited
131 T Len Zell/OSF/Animals Animals/Earth Scenes
131 B F. Stuart Westmorland/Photo Researchers
132 T Stephen Dalton/Photo Researchers
132 B Mark Stouffer/Animals Animals/Earth Scenes
133 T Fritz Polking/Visuals Unlimited
134 T Charlie Ott/Photo Researchers
134 B Paul A. Grecian/Visuals Unlimited
134 B-Inset Andrew Martinez/Photo Researchers
135 C Pat Armstrong/Visuals Unlimited
135 T Courtesy General Motors Corporation/Wieck Photo DataBase
136 B PhotoDisc, Inc.
136 T PhotoDisc, Inc.
138 L Stephen J. Krasemann/Photo Researchers
138 R Robert W. Domm/Visuals Unlimited
138 C Doug Sokell/Visuals Unlimited
139 C Gary Braasch/Tony Stone Images
139 R David Matherly/Visuals Unlimited
139 L Ron Spomer/Visuals Unlimited
140 B-Inset Alan D. Carey/Photo Researchers
140 T Stephen J. Krasemann/Photo Researchers
140 B Jim Zipp/Photo Researchers
141 B E. R. Degginger/Color-Pic, Inc.
141 T Doug Sokell/Visuals Unlimited
142 CC Phil Degginger/Animals Animals/Earth Scenes
142 B North Wind Picture Archives
142 TC Patti Murray/Animals Animals/Earth Scenes
142 T Robert W. Domm/Visuals Unlimited
143 B Andy Sacks/Tony Stone Images
143 T Ron Spomer/Visuals Unlimited

144 T Gary Braasch/Tony Stone Images
144 B Superstock
144 B-INSET Cabisco/Visuals Unlimited
145 TL David Matherly/Visuals Unlimited
145 B E. R. Degginger/Color-Pic, Inc.
145 TR John Chard/Tony Stone Images
148 NASA
152 E. R. Degginger/Color-Pic, Inc.
153 PhotoDisc, Inc.
155 F. Stuart Westmorland/Photo Researchers
156 BL VU/Cabisco/Visuals Unlimited
156 BC VU/Cabisco/Visuals Unlimited
156 BR VU/Cabisco/Visuals Unlimited
157 Michael Fogden/Animals Animals/Earth Scenes
159 B J. Forsdyke/Gene Cox/SPL/Photo Researchers
159 T PhotoDisc, Inc.

Unit B

1 D. Boone/Corbis-Westlight
2 T Vincent O'Bryne/Panoramic Images
2 BL Arie deZanger for Scott Foresman
3 C Nicholas Pinturas/Tony Stone Images
11 T Arthur Tilley/FPG International Corp.
13 Dan McCoy/Rainbow
14 L Richard Megna/Fundamental Photographs
14 R Richard Megna/Fundamental Photographs
15 L Richard Megna/Fundamental Photographs
15 R Richard Megna/Fundamental Photographs
15 C Richard Megna/Fundamental Photographs
15 L Richard Megna/Fundamental Photographs
16 T Jill Birschbach
16 B William Wright/Fundamental Photographs
17 Dr. E. R. Degginger/Color-Pic, Inc.
21 R Randy Green/FPG International LLC
21 L Nancy Sheehan/PhotoEdit
24 James Schwabel/Panoramic Images
28 Randy Green/FPG International LLC
29 NASA/SS/Photo Researchers
33 Steve Satushek/Image Bank
35 Steve Kaufman/Corbis Media
36 NASA
37 Carr Clifton/Minden Pictures
38 David Young-Wolff/PhotoEdit
39 Steve Satushek/Image Bank
42 B Brooks/Brown/SSC/Photo Researchers
43 C Jeremy Burgess/Photo Researchers
50 L Boltin Picture Library
50 R Boltin Picture Library
50 BC Charles D. Winters/Photo Researchers
50 CC John Cancalosi/TOM STACK & ASSOCIATES
53 T Kal's Power Tools
54 UPI/Corbis-Bettmann
55 B Lawrence Migdale/Photo Researchers
56 T E. R. Degginger/NASC/Photo Researchers
56 B Superstock, Inc.
59 PhotoDisc, Inc.
63 TR PhotoDisc, Inc.
63 CL PhotoDisc, Inc.
63 CR PhotoDisc, Inc.
65 T USDA Nature Source/Photo Researchers
66 T Gilbert S. Grant/NASC/Photo Researchers
66 C Michael Boys/Corbis Media
66 B Kevin R. Morris/Corbis Media
67 B Superstock, Inc.
67 T Peter Miller/NASC/Photo Researchers
68 Scott T. Smith/Corbis Media
78 Oxford Scientific Films/Animals Animals/Earth Scenes
79 T Mike Hewitt/Allsport
80 BL Akira Fujii
80 BR Craig J. Brown/Liaison Agency
80 T David Madison/Tony Stone Images
81 Tim Davis/Tony Stone Images
82 L NASA
82 R Akira Fujii
85 John Warden/Tony Stone Images
87 Jose Carrillo/PhotoEdit
88 Mark Wagner/Tony Stone Images
90 Laguna Photo/Liaison Agency
92 Tony Freeman/PhotoEdit
94 N. Pecnik/Visuals Unlimited
95 Jonathan Daniel/Allsport
96 L Don Smetzer/Tony Stone Images

96 R Joe Caputo/Liaison Agency
97 Novastock/PhotoEdit
105 Joseph McBride/Tony Stone Images
106 Jonathan Nourok/PhotoEdit
108 L Dan McCoy/Rainbow
108 R E. R. Degginger/Color-Pic, Inc.
109 T VCG/FPG International Corp.
109 B Jose Carrillo/PhotoEdit
118 Novastock/PhotoEdit
120 Vince Streano/Tony Stone Images
123 PhotoDisc, Inc.
124 Warren Stone/Visuals Unlimited
125 Spencer Grant/Photo Researchers
129 B Scott Camazine/Photo Researchers
129 T Rosenfeld Images LTD/SPL/Photo Researchers
132 David Parker/Photo Researchers
135 B Novastock/PhotoEdit
135 C Jerome Wexler/Photo Researchers
137 B Gregg Hadel/Tony Stone Images
138 R Paul Silverman/Fundamental Photographs
138 L Paul Silverman/Fundamental Photographs
139 T Jeff Greenberg/Visuals Unlimited
139 B Lawrence Migdale/Photo Researchers
143 T Breck P. Kent/Animals Animals/Earth Scenes
143 B Renee Lynn/Photo Researchers
145 Kim Westerskov/Tony Stone Images
146 Oliver Benn/Tony Stone Images
147 NASA/SS/Photo Researchers
148 Ulrike Welsch/Photo Researchers
149 B Sylvain Grandadam/Photo Researchers
150 Background PhotoDisc, Inc.
150 TC Phil McCarten/PhotoEdit
150 CR Corel
150 BL MetaTools
151 TL PhotoDisc, Inc.
151 TR David Young-Wolff/Tony Stone Images
155 Renee Lynn/Photo Researchers
157 UPI/Corbis-Bettmann
159 T PhotoDisc

Unit C

1 Merrilee Thomas/TOM STACK & ASSOCIATES
2 T Vincent O'Bryne/Panoramic Images
2 BL A. Gragera/Latin Stock/SPL/Photo Researchers
2 C Merrilee Thomas/TOM STACK & ASSOCIATES
3 C NASA
3 B Geoff Tompkinson/SPL/Photo Researchers
4 Inset NOAA/TOM STACK & ASSOCIATES
9 T Stephen Ferry/Liaison Agency
9 B NOAA/TOM STACK & ASSOCIATES
13 Gary W. Carter/Visuals Unlimited
15 BL Bayard H. Brattstrom/Visuals Unlimited
15 TR Robert Stahl/Tony Stone Images
15 TL A. J. Copley/Visuals Unlimited
15 BR Lincoln Nutting/Photo Researchers
17 Frank Oberle/Tony Stone Images
18 The Newberry Library/Stock Montage
19 Granger Collection
20 C Christian Grzimek/Okapia/Photo Researchers
20 Background PhotoDisc, Inc.
21 T Dr. E. R. Degginger/Color-Pic, Inc.
21 Background PhotoDisc
22 B Joyce Photographics/Photo Researchers
22 T Davis Instruments
23 Howard Bluestein/Photo Researchers
24 B David Parker/ESA/SPL/Photo Researchers
24 T TSADO/NCDC/NASA/TOM STACK & ASSOCIATES
25 T TSADO/NCDC/NASA/TOM STACK & ASSOCIATES"
30 Courtesy of NOAA Photo Library
32 Charles Doswell III/Tony Stone Images
34 Wetmore/Photo Researchers
35 T Alan R. Moller/Tony Stone Images
35 B Dan McCoy/Rainbow
36 L NASA/SPL/Photo Researchers
36 R R. Perron/Visuals Unlimited
37 Alan R. Moller/Tony Stone Images
39 TSADO/NCDC/NASA/TOM STACK & ASSOCIATES
46 L Francois Gohier/SSC/Photo Researchers

46 R Alison Wright/NASC/Photo Researchers
46 C Glenn Oliver/Visuals Unlimited
47 R Eye Ubiquitous/Corbis Media
48 U. S. Geological Survey
49 (c) Michael L. Smith
50 T Corbis/Ressmeyer
50 B Paulus Leeser
51 B David Parker/SPL/SSC/Photo Researchers
51 T U. S. Geological Survey
56 C William E. Ferguson
56 R William E. Ferguson
56 L Corel
57 B Superstock, Inc.
57 T U. S. Geological Survey/EROS Data Center
58 Carr Clifton/Minden Pictures
59 B Ray Fairbanks/NASC/Photo Researchers
59 T Frans Lanting/Minden Pictures
61 PhotoDisc, Inc.
62 Superstock, Inc.
63 PhotoDisc, Inc.
64 Superstock, Inc.
65 L Larry Blank/Visuals Unlimited
65 R Carr Clifton/Minden Pictures
68 Background Joe McDonald/Visuals Unlimited
68 Inset Ross Frid/Visuals Unlimited
69 BL A. J. Copley/Visuals Unlimited
69 BR John D. Cunningham/Visuals Unlimited
70 Tom Bean
71 BCR A. J. Copley/Visuals Unlimited
71 T Layne Kennedy/Corbis Media
71 CR James L. Amos/Corbis Media
71 TCL Wolfgang Kaehler/Corbis Media
71 TCR Layne Kennedy/Corbis Media
71 BCL Tom Bean/Corbis Media
71 B A. J. Copley/Visuals Unlimited
72 BL Copyright (c) Peabody Museum of Natural
   History, Yale University, New Haven,
   Connecticut. Painting by Shirley G. Hartman
73 T David M. Dennis/TOM STACK &
   ASSOCIATES
73 B Layne Kennedy/Corbis Media
77 Wolfgang Kaehler/Corbis Media
78 Photo courtesy of U. S. space camp (c) U. S.
   Space & Rocket Center
83 Background Jay Pasachoff/Visuals Unlimited
83 Inset ESA/TSADO/TOM STACK &
   ASSOCIATES
87 Jeff Greenberg/MR/Visuals Unlimited
89 B SCIENCE VU/Visuals Unlimited
89 TR Tersch Enterprises
90 T NASA
90 B Johnny Johnson/Tony Stone Images
91 C USNO/TSADO/TOM STACK &
   ASSOCIATES
91 R United States Naval Observatory
91 L Science VU/Visuals Unlimited
93 The Association of Universities for Research III
101 T Simon Fraser/SPL/Photo Researchers
101 BL NASA
101 BR NASA
102 BR NASA
102 CL NASA
103 T Dept. of Clinical Radiology, Salisbury
   District Hospital/SPLPhoto Researchers
103 C Custom Medical Stock Photo
104 TL Sovfoto/Eastfoto
104 BC UPI/Corbis-Bettmann
104 CR NASA
104 BR PhotoDisc, Inc.
104 Background Ed Degginger/Color-Pic, Inc.
105 TL NASA
105 TR E. R. Degginger/Color-Pic, Inc.
105 BR NASA
107 NASA
113 BR Karl Gehring/Liaison Agency
114 T SuperStock, Inc.
114 BL SuperStock, Inc.
114 BR Jonathan Nourok/PhotoEdit
115 Tess Young/TOM STACK & ASSOCIATES
116 L PhotoDisc, Inc.
116 R PhotoDisc, Inc.
117 CL MetaPhotos
117 T SuperStock, Inc.
117 BL MetaPhotos
117 BR MetaPhotos

117 BC PhotoDisc, Inc.
118 PhotoDisc, Inc.
118 B-inset SuperStock, Inc.
120 T Institute of Oceanographic
   Sciences/NERC/SPL/Photo Researchers
120 BR John Moss/Photo Researchers
120 BL MetaTools
121 Dr. Ken MacDonald/SPL/Photo Researchers
122 BL Stephen J. Krasemann/Photo Researchers
123 Background PhotoDisc, Inc.
123 BL PhotoDisc, Inc.
123 BR Corel
123 TL D. P. Wilson/Photo Researchers
123 C Gregory Ochocki/Photo Researchers
124 PhotoDisc, Inc.
125 TR PhotoDisc, Inc.
125 CL Corel
125 CR Dana White/PhotoEdit
125 B Barbara Stitzer/PhotoEdit
128 L National Museum of American
   Art/Smithsonian Institution
128 R The Granger Collection, New York
129 BL Corel
129 C Library of Congress
129 BR PhotoDisc, Inc.
130 BL Library of Congress
130 BC UPI/Corbis-Bettmann
130 BR Federal Duck Stamp Program/U.S. Fish &
   Wildlife Service
131 BL UPI/Corbis-Bettmann
131 BC UPI/Corbis-Bettmann
132 BL UPI/Corbis-Bettmann
132 BR David R. Frazier/Tony Stone Images
133 BL Joe Traver/New York Times/Archive
   Photos
133 BC Kaku Kurita/Liaison Agency
133 BR Courtesy General Motors
   Corporation/Wieck Photo DataBase
134 Jeff Isaac Greenberg/Photo Researchers
139 SuperStock, Inc.
140 Alan R. Moller/Tony Stone Images
141 TSADO/NCDC/NASA/TOM STACK &
   ASSOCIATES
142 T PhotoDisc, Inc.
144 NASA

Unit D
1 Chris Trotman/Duomo Photography Inc.
2 T Vincent O'Bryne/Panoramic Images
2 C-Inset Dan McCoy/Rainbow
3 B Weinberg-Clark/Image Bank
3 C Hank Morgan/Photo Researchers
7 David M. Philips/Visuals Unlimited
12 Matthew Stockman/Allsport
13 Stephen McBrady/PhotoEdit
14 Ralph C. Eagle, Jr., MD/Photo Researchers
15 T Tony Duffy/Allsport
15 C Prof. P. Motta/Dept. of Anatomy/University
   "La Sapienza", Rome/SPL/Photo Researchers
16 C Omikron/Photo Researchers
16 T PhotoDisc, Inc.
17 Mary Kate Denny/PhotoEdit
21 David M. Philips/Visuals Unlimited
22 Brian Bahr/Allsport
25 Express/Archive Photos
30 Mary Kate Denny/PhotoEdit
37 PhotoDisc, Inc.
38 Hank Morgan/SS/Photo Researchers
39 T Charles O. Cecil/Visuals Unlimited
44 David Pollack/Stock Market
45 Inset Fred Hossler/Visuals Unlimited
46 B Martin Rotker/Phototake
46 T Martin Rotker/Phototake
47 L Barts Medical Library/Phototake
47 R Barts Medical Library/Phototake
49 PhotoDisc, Inc.
50 SPL/Photo Researchers
54 T Martin M. Rotker/Photo Researchers
54 b SIU/Photo Researchers
55 Rafael Macia/Photo Researchers
56 Larry Mulvehill/Photo Researchers
60 Brian Bahr/Allsport
61 David Pollack/Stock Market
63 T PhotoDisc, Inc.
63 B PhotoDisc, Inc.

End Matter

Illustration
20 J/B Woolsey
32 J/B Woolsey
33 Meryl Treatner
34 T Corel
34 BL Corel
34 BR A. J. Copley/Visuals Unlimited
35 J/B Woolsey
36 J/B Woolsey
37 J/B Woolsey
38 Joel Ito
39 Joel Ito
42 Ovresat Parades Design
43 Ovresat Parades Design

Photography
4 B Bob Kalmbach, University of Michigan Photo
   Services
10 L PhotoDisc, Inc.
10 R PhotoDisc, Inc.
30 BL Oliver Meckes/SPL/SSC/Photo Researchers
30 TL Stan Flegler/Visuals Unlimited
30 TC J. Forsdyke/Gene Cox/SPL/Photo
   Researchers
30 BR MetaTools
30 CR Bob and Clara Calhoun/Bruce Coleman
   Inc.
30 TR Joe McDonald/Animals Animals/Earth
   Scenes
34 T Corel
34 CR A. J. Copley/Visuals Unlimited
34 BL Corel
45 B NOAO/Lowell Observatory
45 T Alinari/Art Resource, NY
46 T Trinity College Library, Cambridge
46 B The Granger Collection, New York
47 R National Library of Medicine
47 L From "The Structure of the Human Body,"
   1543
48 B Metropolitan Museum of Art
48 T British Museum
48 TL National Museum of Women in the Arts,
   Washington, DC
48 TR From Robert Hooke, "Micrographia," 1665
48 C Public Domain
49 B London School of Hygiene & Tropical
   Medicine/SPL/Photo Researchers
49 TR Genera Plantarum, Leiden 1737/Public
   Domain
49 C JPL/NASA
49 TL Public Domain
50 TL James L. Amos/Photo Researchers
50 TR Hugh Spencer
50 c Mehau Kulyk/SPL/Photo Researchers
50 B David Frazier/Photo Researchers
51 T Courtesy Mr. G. P. Darwin, by permission of
   the Darwin Museum, Down House
51 C Courtesy Southern Pacific Railroad
51 B Harvard Medical Library, Francis A.
   Countway Library of Medicine
52 L PhotoDisc, Inc.
52 R UPI/Corbis-Bettmann
53 T Staatliches Museum fur Naturkunde,
   Stuttgart
53 C Charles D. Winters/Timeframe Photography
   Inc./Photo Researchers
53 B UPI/Corbis-Bettmann
54 T Tim Davis/Photo Researchers
54 C NASA
54 BL The Granger Collection, New York
55 T AP/Wide World
55 TC Computer Museum, Boston
55 CL Tim Shaffer/AP/Wide World
55 CR
55 BL Scott Camazine/Photo Researchers
55 BR NASA
57 B AP/Wide World